A
time
to
kill

Other titles by the same author:

Blood on the Thistle
Frightener (with Lisa Brownlie)
No Final Solution

A TIME TO KILL

DOUGLAS SKELTON

MAINSTREAM
PUBLISHING

EDINBURGH AND LONDON

First published in Great Britain in 1995 by
MAINSTREAM PUBLISHING COMPANY (EDINBURGH) LTD
7 Albany Street
Edinburgh EH1 3UG

ISBN 1 85158 721 7

A catalogue record for this book is available from the British Library

Typeset in Palatino by Litho Link Ltd, Welshpool, Powys, Wales
Printed and bound in Great Britain by Butler & Tanner Ltd, Frome

Contents

Acknowledgments

THANKS, as ever, are due to the following people without whom this book would never have seen the light of day:

Stephen Wilkie of the *Daily Record* for the endless stream of information;

Russell Kyle and Russell Leadbetter, Glasgow *Evening Times* for their help;

Mark Sweeney of the *Scottish Sun* for the pictures;

Martin Jones for looking over the manuscript and for his always helpful comments;

John Carroll for his advice and assistance;

Stanley Leech for the photography;

Bill Arthur for allowing us to take over his home;

the bosses and staff at Mainstream for putting up with my disorganisation;

Chris Bell for making an honest woman of Katie.

Shots in the Dark

THE DECEMBER MAN

IN THE DAYS AND months immediately following the end of the Second World War, Britain's cities experienced a crime wave of unparalleled proportions.

The country was inundated with demobbed service men and deserters, not just from Britain's forces but from those of its allies. Then there were the refugees who had fled their homes before the Nazi onslaught in Europe and had reached the safety of these shores. Most of these soldiers, sailors, airmen and civilians were, of course, law-abiding and were either waiting for their chance to return to their homes in the bombed-out cities of Europe, or for permission to settle in this country.

However, there were a few who chose to indulge in crime. Theft, extortion, rape and murder became so common after the end of hostilities that Scotland Yard cancelled all leave for officers in order to enforce a crackdown in the south of England. Police forces throughout Britain faced similar problems.

An added element was the number of firearms and ammunition available through the black market as returning soldiers made some quick cash by off-loading liberated weapons to their friendly, local criminal.

It was one such weapon that was used in a double murder in the Empire's second city in 1945.

Before the days of smokeless fuel, when the cities were still heavily industrialised and countless factory chimneys belched out thick dark smoke day in and day out, fog was a way of life.

The thick greyish brown substance that regularly enveloped Glasgow, Edinburgh and Dundee was not like the soft mists we experience today. It was a mixture of natural mists and the black smoke from thousands of household and commercial chimneys – or lums – which eventually came to be called 'smog'. It would descend on the cities like a noxious blanket; the taste of soot permeating every breath and clinging round streetlamps until visibility was often cut down to a matter of inches. Pollution may not yet have been on everyone's lips, but it was certainly down their throats and in their lungs.

It was a peasouper like this that draped itself over Glasgow on Monday, 10 December 1945, and acted as a shield for a gunman to murder two people and wound another.

It was about 7.40 p.m. and the fog wrapped itself around Pollokshields East Station on the city's Cathcart circle line like a grey poultice; soaking up what little light there was, forcing trains to run a little late. Somewhere in the gloom, two street musicians were playing Christmas carols, the seasonal sounds floating eerily through the smog and into the gaslit station-master's office, where a coal fire crackled warmly in the grate.

There were three members of staff on duty that night – William Wright, the porter-clerk; clerkess Annie Withers and porter Robert Gough. The three were talking away happily as they huddled round the fire, waiting for the next train to arrive. The war was over and they had been promised a better world. Christmas was coming and they had everything to live for.

The first sign of the impending terror was when Robert Gough saw the flash of a face at the office window. He only had time to register the paleness of the man's skin, then it was gone again. He did not even have the chance to comment on it before the door opened and the dark shape of a man could be seen framed in the doorway, a hat pulled down low over his eyes, his body bundled up in a long coat.

And in his hand was a pistol.

All he said was, 'This is a hold up!' Annie Withers rose to her feet and screamed. The man fired at her, then swivelled the pistol to fire at the two men as he spotted young Robert Gough moving.

The boy slumped to the floor, a slug catching his right arm and then lodging in his abdomen. William Wright felt a bullet graze his right side and then he too collapsed.

As he fell, he could still hear the clerkess screaming; then the gunman turned round and fired at her twice more. The woman stopped screaming and fell on to her back, blood streaming from her wounds. The first bullet had embedded itself in her left thigh after having cut through her left arm. The next caught her on the chest, erupting out again under her left armpit, while the third entered by her stomach and careered through her body, leaving a gaping exit hole on her back.

The porter-clerk was too shocked to move after that. He could hear Miss Withers groaning in pain and Robert Gough's laboured breathing, but there was nothing he could do. If he had moved, the man would only have shot him again anyway.

The gunman calmly stepped over the bodies and began to rifle through the drawers of the safe. Then he ran out of the station and into the night; the thick fog wrapping around him like a shroud.

No one saw him arrive and no one saw him leave. The only witnesses were the three wounded people lying on the office floor behind him.

And all the while, the muffled notes of the musicians' carols wafted into the silent night.

Finally, Wright felt able to move. He pulled himself to the station's telephone and contacted the signal box some distance away across the tracks. He told the signalman there had been a shooting and asked him to get help. Then he returned to try and somehow assist the wounded Annie Withers.

It was as he was placing a folded-up coat under her head that he heard a train approaching the station. He moved sluggishly out of the office and saw the guard climbing from his cabin. Wright told him that there had been a shooting, but the guard did not believe him. He laughed at what he thought was a joke on the porter-clerk's part and whistled to the engine driver to pull out of the station. The locomotive puffed away from the scene of the crime, the guard no doubt shaking his head at the wild story. A shooting indeed . . .

However, had he looked behind William Wright he would have seen the proof of the man's story. Robert Gough had come

11

round and had crawled out on to the platform, where he lay bleeding from the wounds in his arm and belly.

The signalman Wright had telephoned believed the tale, however, and alerted the police. Two officers shortly arrived with other rail workers, shock registering as they came upon the carnage in the small office. An ambulance was called to take the wounded to hospital.

Thirty-six-year-old Annie Withers did not make it. She died on the way to the Victoria Infirmary.

Robert Gough was slipping in and out of consciousness. Detectives sat by his bedside for 36 hours, each time he opened his eyes trying to obtain a fuller description of the gunman.

Finally, by putting together what they had gleaned from both men, the police were able to announce that they were looking for a man between 30 and 35 years, was about five foot, seven inches tall with a very white, clean-shaven face, had ginger hair, and was wearing a light linen raincoat of the type issued to demobbed soldiers, and a light-grey or light-brown soft-felt hat. It wasn't much to go on, but it was all they would get. Gough and Wright had only seen the man fleetingly, and then only in the light of two gas lamps. And no one had seen him either arrive or leave.

On Tuesday, 12 December, Robert Gough succumbed to his wounds in hospital. He was only 15 years of age.

He was buried the following Sunday in Eastwood New Cemetery. Hundred of mourners watched as his coffin was lowered into the ground, among them the boy's father, representatives of the railroad company and William Wright – now the only surviving witness. A bugler from the Howe Sea Cadet Unit, of which the dead youth was a member, plaintively blew 'The Last Post' over the grave; each pause in the lament punctuated by sobs from the crowd.

Annie Withers had been buried by her parents two days before in her native Galston in Ayrshire. Mr Wright and company managers also attended that service.

They had died so that the gunman could get away with one packet containing a signalman's wage of just over four pounds.

Meanwhile, Glasgow police had cast a massive dragnet across the country to catch the killer. Inquiries took them to Oban, where a red-headed man had been spotted getting off the night train from Glasgow in an agitated state and showing a great interest in the news of the murders in the morning paper. But this man was eventually traced and cleared.

In Glasgow, officers were rounding up people in illegal possession of handguns. They gathered a collection of such weapons, including a German-made Luger 9mm with 92 rounds of ammunition. But none of them proved to be the murder weapon.

Men with red or ginger hair were stopped and questioned. Where were they on the night of the tenth? Who were they with? Could they prove it? Did they own a gun? But they did not find the right man. Maybe he wasn't even ginger-haired after all – it was pretty dingy in that office. Maybe it just looked red.

Then someone with apparent knowledge of the crime wrote to Glasgow CID, signing the letter with the word 'right'. Detectives arranged for the *Daily Record* to print a special box on the front page of their Saturday, 15 December edition in which the word figured prominently, hoping that the letter-writer would get in contact again.

Again, nothing happened.

Glasgow Corporation announced a reward of £1,000 for information leading to the arrest of the killer. The plan was to take the money out of the police fund. However, the Lord Advocate would not sanction the use of police grant money in that way, while the Secretary of State for Scotland said that if the authority wanted to put up the cash, then they must find it themselves. That would mean the money would have to come from the ratepayers; the corporation were forced to have second thoughts. Eventually, the *Scottish Daily Express* pledged the reward. But no one came forward with any information which would lead the police to the culprit.

The murderer, whoever he was, had vanished into the fog that night like a wraith; leaving no trail, no clues, no hints as to his identity – apart from three fingerprints on the office safe; fingerprints which could not be matched with any on file. It was as if he never existed.

Ten months passed. The story of the murders in the station died. Other events took up newspaper columns and the public mind; other crimes kept the police busy. Then, on 8 October 1946, two detectives called at the home of a Charles Templeman Brown on the southside of Glasgow and spoke to his mother. They had received a tip-off that the man was in possession of a Luger, although, naturally, they did not tell her that. They said they just wanted to speak to him. It was a routine matter.

Charles wasn't at home, the woman told them. He was a railway fireman and was away that day on a long run. The two men glanced at each other – the fact that he was a railway worker no doubt registering – and asked the woman to have her son contact them when he returned.

The woman duly passed the message on to her son on his return from work and the following day the 20-year-old, fair-haired Brown approached a constable who was directing traffic on Newlands Road, in the Cathcart area of Glasgow, and asked him, 'Will you phone Central for me?' When asked by the officer why he wanted him to phone the police headquarters, Brown simply replied, 'I did a murder.' The policeman's eyebrows shot up and Brown added, 'the Pollokshields job.'

Murder obviously taking precedence over the smooth flow of traffic, the officer took Brown to a police box in nearby Spean Street, where Brown gave him a 1918 Luger and a small box containing 13 rounds of ammunition. The policeman placed Brown in the box while he waited for senior officers to arrive. While inside, Brown used a police message-pad to scribble a note to a friend in the Highland Light Infantry. The note read:

> Dear Bill,
>
> I know you will be very surprised to learn that I have given myself up for the Pollokshields murder. Remember how on your last leave we discussed it? Little did you know it was I.
>
> I tried to kill myself this morning, but when I pulled the trigger, it would not fire, yet a second later it fired when pointed at the river.
>
> After a while I fell asleep and woke knowing I must give myself up. I hope by this rotten crime I have not lost your friendship.
>
> C. Brown.

The constable contacted Southern Division CID and when Detective Sergeant Murdoch McKenzie arrived to pick Brown up from the police box, the young man told him, 'I didn't mean to kill anyone, but once you start shooting you can't stop.'

He later added, 'I would have been walking about dressed today if yon wee boy had not dived at me.'

However, before he died, Robert Gough had made a dying deposition to a Sheriff in which he had stated he had moved only to protect Annie Withers from the bullets. He had not been diving at Brown at all.

When searched by DS McKenzie, Brown was found to be carrying a slip of paper wedged inside a book of railway rules. On it was written in Brown's handwriting:

> I am not sorry for anything I did, only for the things I did not do. Goodbye, good luck to Billy McKay and you.
>
> C. Brown

Brown's fingerprints were taken and the prints on three fingers of his right hand matched those lifted from the handles of the railway-office safe and a tin box. The gun he had handed to the traffic officer was tested and found to be the one which had fired the shots almost a year before. William Wright was called to an identification parade and picked out Brown immediately from the line-up. 'His face has remained in my memory ever since that night,' he said later.

The day after his arrest, Brown took police to the spot beside the River Cart where, he claimed, he had made his obviously unsuccessful suicide attempt. They found two empty cartridge cases and two live rounds.

Everything had fallen into place. They had the murder weapon. They had a confession. They had corroboration in William Wright's identification and the fingerprint evidence. Now all they needed was a conviction and Brown would be facing the hangman.

For the second time in Brown's young life, the date 10 December had telling significance. It was on 10 December 1945 that he made his violent raid on the railway station. And it was exactly one year later that his trial began in the High Court of Glasgow.

The five-day trial was heard by Lord Carmont, arguably one of the most severe Scottish judges of the century. It was his draconian sentences against the city's street gangs which led the accused to complain about 'copping a Carmont'. Prosecuting was advocate-deputy, Mr John Wheatley, who was later to become Lord Wheatley and a judge of some repute. Defending Brown was

15

Mr John Cameron, KC, who, as Lord Cameron, would also become a judge.

Throughout the proceedings, Charles Templeman Brown sat calmly listening to the evidence against him. Author Bill Knox, then a young reporter, covered the case, and in his book *Court of Murder* (John Long, 1968) he said that the accused often seemed disinterested in what was happening around him. There was little the defence could do about the weight of evidence against Brown. He had, it would seem, been firmly placed in that small, gaslit room on that foggy night, with the gun in his hand. Instead, they concentrated on Brown's psychological state. It may be the only case where a fascination with swing music would play a strong role in the defence of a murderer.

The first suggestion of this came in the second day when the Crown called a 24-year-old student friend of the accused, who told the court that in February 1946, Brown had confessed to him that he had committed the double murder; suggesting that by turning him in, the student could earn himself the thousand pound reward. But Brown was something of a storyteller and a fantasist and the student – along with the other people to whom Brown confessed at this time – did not pay much attention.

Under cross-examination, the student said that Brown had taken intense interest in a number of subjects, naming Communism as an example. He loved the music of bandleader Joe Loss and became a follower of Frank Sinatra, described in court as 'a well-known American crooner' – even to the extent of dressing like him in bow ties and camel-hair jackets.

Brown's mother confirmed this fascination. She said he had previously shown such interest in Joseph Stalin and Adolf Hitler. Then it had switched to swing music and, in particular, Frank Sinatra. It was, it seems, an attraction which bordered on idolatry. On one momentous occasion, Brown even travelled the 500 miles to London in order to buy a white whipcord jacket similar to the type worn by the singer. Such a journey may not be unusual today, but in the 1940s it was practically unheard of. After all, as a railway fireman, Brown only earned £4 per week. So proud was Brown of this jacket that on occasion he would leave work on a Friday without picking up his pay packet, go home, put it on and return to collect his wage.

Mrs Brown also said that her son had been experiencing sharp mood swings for two years, being irritable one day and cheerful the next. Sometimes, she said, he would not speak for hours.

Dr William Blyth, physician in charge of mental and nervous diseases at Glasgow's Royal Infirmary, said that he had examined Brown twice in Barlinnie Prison and was of the opinion that the accused was suffering from incipient dementia praecox – a form of schizophrenia. He said he did not think it abnormal for a person to want to wear bow ties, although, in his opinion, it may be abnormal for someone in Glasgow to wear a white whipcord jacket. However, it was Brown's advocacy of violence and his tendency to fantasise that really made him think he was suffering from a mental disorder. But when asked if he would be prepared to certify Brown as insane, the doctor replied, 'Medically, yes. Legally, no.'

Another expert, Dr Ivy McKenzie, had examined Brown five times since his arrest and although he conceded that the accused was fit to plead, he did feel he was mentally unstable. 'I was impressed first of all with the ease and indifference with which he took the situation in which he found himself,' he observed.

In his final speech to the jury, Mr Wheatley said that the opinions of the medical experts called by the defence should be rejected, pointing out that because a man wore extravagant clothing did not make him mentally abnormal. Mr Cameron countered by saying that if they found his client guilty then it should not be of murder, but of culpable homicide because of Brown's mental state.

The judge told the jury that they must make their own mind up as men and women of the world. This is perfectly correct – judges must point this out, nowadays generally using the phrase, 'You are the masters of the facts. You must decide.' However, they can register their own view about a certain piece of evidence by an intonation in their voice or a facial expression, and, for some reason, Lord Carmont saw fit to tell the jury to dismiss aspects of the medical experts' evidence, saying that they had a tendency to over-emphasise things that fell within their sphere.

The jury was out for an hour. They filed back into the jury bench and announced that they had found Brown guilty of murder and robbery. Brown's mother fainted when she heard the jury's verdict and had to be carried out of the courtroom. She did not see Lord Carmont place the black cap on his head or hear him say that

Brown would be taken from this place and, on 3 January 1947, in Barlinnie Prison, would be hanged by the neck until dead.

Brown appeared to be unmoved by the prospect of dangling at the end of a rope. After the judge pronounced the death sentence, Brown calmly turned away and disappeared down the stairs to the cells below; still no trace of emotion on his face.

An appeal was promptly lodged. Days passed. Christmas came and went. Then, on 30 December, while the city outside the damp grey walls of the Glasgow prison prepared for the New Year festivities, Charles Templeman Brown was visited in the condemned cell by a senior magistrate and a city official who told him that the Secretary of State for Scotland had commuted his sentence to one of life imprisonment. He would not be judicially murdered after all.

In 1957, Charles Templeman Brown was released from prison and promptly found work as a travelling salesman for a Glasgow tyre-firm. For the next three years he led an unremarkable life. His case was largely forgotten by then, having been overtaken by the horrors perpetrated by the likes of Peter Manuel.

Then one night in 1960, as he was driving on the A9 near Dunblane, his hired car left the road and ploughed through a wall. His passenger, a 21-year-old woman, was slightly injured. Brown was killed outright.

The date was 10 December . . .

Firearms, like the poor, are always with us, it seems. For despite regular attempts by police and governments to crack down on the spread of illegal weapons – weapons that are held legally are another matter entirely – there always seems to be plenty to be had. Shotguns, as ever, are the big favourite. They are, after all, easily obtainable. Most farmers have at least one, for instance, while gun-shops can be raided if the need arises. Revolvers and automatic handguns are also very popular among criminals and are becoming more and more common on city streets as rival gangs wage war. Even imitations, which are quite freely available, can be used in any criminal enterprise.

But if a criminal has it in mind to do a 'turn' – in other words, pull a job, like a bank raid – he can arm himself with a rented weapon. Prices vary, depending on the type and quality of weapon needed, and if the firearm is actually used during the turn then it is said that it is broken up and never used again.

Another type of weapon becoming increasingly apparent in the cities are the deactivated firearms which have been restored by experts to full firing condition. In 1991, police officers came upon an arsenal of various weapons stashed in a cemetery in Barlanark – a somewhat notorious housing scheme in the far east of Glasgow. Nestling among the usual sawn-off shotguns and pistols was an officially deactivated South African kommando semi-automatic machine-pistol. This lightweight, ugly and quite lethal pistol had been restored so that it could once again fire its full load of 25 rounds. Deactivated weapons are available via mail order and enthusiasts claim that it is not possible for them to be reactivated. But the fact that they *can* be restored to their formal lethal glory is testified by the kommando found in that Glasgow graveyard, as well as other similar weapons found since.

The find also exemplified another disturbing trend – that Glasgow's criminals, at least, engaged as they were in a drug war, were no longer satisfied with the more traditional weapons, and were looking for guns which were more effective and more lethal. The famed Russian-made kalashnikov, and copies thereof, has made a number of appearances on the streets, perhaps most tellingly in a case from November 1991 when a man was told to kill by evil voices.

Glasgow man Noel Ruddle had been given the Chinese copy of Professor Kalashnikov's creation in a pub, by former soldier Edward Molloy, who had brought it into the country after serving during the Gulf War. Molloy, subsequently sentenced to two years for smuggling, asked Ruddle to sell it for him.

What he did not know was that Ruddle was mentally un-balanced. He heard voices and the voices told him to do things. He called the voices – two male and two female – 'the evil set' and, shortly after he took possession of the weapon, they told him that everyone was plotting against him and he should kill them all.

Ruddle had already been drinking heavily when neighbours James McConville and John Stevenson asked him if he wished to buy some more from them. He said he did and they returned to his flat in the high-rise block at Queen Elizabeth Square in the Gorbals.

The two men waited at Ruddle's door as he went inside to pick up some money.

But it was not money he brought out to them – it was the kalashnikov copy. John Stevenson took to his heels immediately and Ruddle fired off a round at him, missing him completely. Unfortunately McConville did not react quickly enough. Ruddle turned on him and shot him through the liver.

After that, he began firing shots from the windows into the streets below, narrowly missing two 14-year-old schoolgirls who heard the bullets from the rifle – which has a range of up to two and a half miles – ricocheting from the pavement around them. One bullet smashed through a car windscreen and wedged in the gearbox, luckily, it did not hit the driver.

Armed police officers converged on the Gorbals square but Ruddle held them at bay for a full eight hours before finally giving himself up. Ruddle was diagnosed as suffering from paranoia and having a split personality, and in March 1992 he pled guilty to a charge of culpable homicide (known in England and Wales as manslaughter) due to diminished responsibility. He was ordered to be detained at Carstairs State Hospital without limit of time.

Three years later he hit the headlines again, when staff at the hospital, suspicious of what they called his 'lippy' attitude and fearing he had been taking unauthorised drugs, searched his room and found supplies of whisky and vodka. A search of a locker he used in the hospital's education room revealed a supply of 'sulph', or amphetamine sulphate. Nurses told reporters that such a haul could have given Ruddle unlimited purchasing power within the hospital. The amount of sulph found in the locker could even have given him the power to pay for the murder of a fellow patient or a member of staff. And with the horrific escape attempt by Robert Mone and Thomas McCulloch in 1976 still fresh in their minds – as well as other more recent incidents – the staff were very concerned about this breach of security.

Ruddle was immediately transferred to another ward while an investigation was launched to find out just how the drink and drugs came into his possession. Then, within days, another scandal rocked the hospital, as it was revealed that a woman worker had allegedly sent explicit sex letters to Ruddle, who was described as a 'smooth-talking psychopath'.

Meanwhile, a kalashnikov was among a haul of weapons found in the Aberdeen flat of a so-called Tartan Terrorist. Andrew McIntosh was arrested by Grampian police in 1993 and subsequently found guilty of conspiring to further the aims of the Scottish National Liberation Army through criminal means. He was also found guilty of sending a variety of letter bombs – including one to Anglian Water in the Prime Minister's Huntingdon constituency which injured a secretary when opened, and also a number of hoax bomb threats which paralysed the city centres of Edinburgh and Glasgow for a day. When police finally tracked him down and raided his flat, they found not just the kalashnikov but various other automatic weapons and a quantity of CS gas.

Another Russian-made weapon, a shotgun this time, was part of a case which proves that it is not just the so-called lower classes who can fall from grace. In Aberdeen, in 1994, two ex-public schoolboys planned crime for kicks, robbing a bank and planning a wages snatch.

Paul Macklin, then aged 21, met Robert Cadiz, aged 22, at Aberdeen's Robert Gordon's College. They both came from fairly privileged backgrounds – Macklin's family owned a personnel company and a perfume store, while Cadiz's father was an oil company executive – and they both had a passion for outdoor pursuits and flash cars. Macklin, a former pupil of 'top people's school' Gordonstoun, would often boast about his feats, including one where he skied off a mountain and parachuted the remainder of the way down.

Together they planned armed robberies – because, it was suggested, they were both 'adrenalin junkies who glorified violence'. They were caught after a wage snatch went wrong and Macklin threatened four police officers with a loaded shotgun before trying to escape in a hijacked car. They had planned to make off with over £300,000 from a van delivering wages to Aberdeen District Council workers. But a passer-by saw the two young men acting suspiciously and reported them to the police. Macklin turned the gun on the officers then forced his way into a passing car and forced the driver at gunpoint to drive off.

He was eventually caught and sentenced to eight years in prison for his crimes, while Cadiz was given nine years. Cadiz was found guilty of robbing a bank at gunpoint and making off with £3,000.

It was a handgun, the most powerful handgun in the world if Dirty Harry is to be believed, which brought terror to a Lanarkshire street in 1993 during an attempted robbery which left one man dead but made heroes out of three other people.

It was on 19 May that 27-year-old Raymond McCourt, from Granton in Edinburgh, walked into the shop of newsagent Khalid Mahmood in Main Street, Cambuslang, and shot him in the face at point-blank range with a .44 Magnum before helping himself to £90 in cash from the till and a quantity of cigarettes from the shelves. Then, as the 37-year-old shopkeeper lay dying on the floor behind his counter with a bullet lodged in his brain, McCourt ran into the bakery next door, demanding more cash from counter staff.

Owner James Kerr had been working in the back shop when he heard the commotion and he moved out front to see what was going on. McCourt turned the gun on him, aiming it at his chest. Without really thinking what he was doing, the baker risked a bluff, telling McCourt that there were police outside and, when the gunman fell for the feint and turned round to see for himself, Kerr lashed out with one of the two rolling-pins he had in his hands, hitting McCourt over the head. McCourt slumped down and then began to rise, still holding the gun, yelling that it was real. But the baker merely hit him again and the would-be robber ran out of his shop with only £12 for his trouble.

But someone had seen him standing in the bakery and had run across the road to Cambuslang police station, then a tiny office on the bottom level of the shopping centre.

The first officer to arrive on the scene was Constable Brian Williams. By this time McCourt had gone into the Sefton Bar nearby and the officer, who, as yet, had no idea that the man was armed, made his way there. When McCourt came out of the pub, he spotted the policeman and drew his weapon, firing it before beginning to run. The first bullet missed, although passers-by threw themselves to the ground in panic.

But the police officer continued his pursuit and finally, near the Savoy Bingo Hall, McCourt whirled round and shouted at the constable, 'Are you fucking crazy?' He raised the gun again and was ready to fire when a woman – 52-year-old Mrs Moira Rooney – who was standing close by shouted, 'Don't shoot the policeman!' McCourt turned the Magnum on her and shot at her; the bullet penetrating her left ankle and into her right lower leg. But she had saved the police officer's life.

The police officer thought, 'To hell with this. I'm going after him,' and launched himself forward again. But McCourt spun back to confront him, pulled the gun up to face-level and fired at him. Constable Williams stopped and instinctively raised his left hand to his own face. Miraculously, the bullet rebounded off his wrist-watch and buried itself in his hand. He was only ten feet away from the crazed gunman. It was his second lucky escape in as many minutes.

McCourt was about to take flight again but realised that Williams was planning to follow. He stopped and turned the gun back on to the wounded officer, warning him, 'Follow me and you're dead.'

The officer made it look as if he was following this advice and tended to the injured Mrs Rooney while McCourt ran off into a lane. He showed the woman his own bleeding hand and tried to comfort her by telling her it was only an air-gun. Then he went after McCourt again, but lost him.

McCourt was later caught after armed police surrounded a house in Westburn Road, Cambuslang. He refused to surrender and they eventually forced their way in. There were no more casualties.

Meanwhile, Mr Mahmood was rushed to hospital but did not show any signs of life. Two days after the robbery, doctors turned off his life-support system. Mrs Rooney spent seven weeks in hospital while Constable Williams was off work for four months following the shootings.

Raymond McCourt pled guilty to murdering and robbing Mr Mahmood; threatening and robbing the bakery staff; discharging the gun at Constable Williams and attempting to murder him and also to shooting Mrs Rooney. He was sentenced to life in prison, with an order that he should serve at least 18 years. In his defence, counsel said that he had been abused as a child and this had left him with emotional and psychological problems.

In June 1994, Mrs Rooney and Mr Kerr were commended for their bravery by Strathclyde police. The two civilians were similarly praised in October 1994 when they were among 100 Scots honoured for their courage and initiative in helping the police.

There was more courage shown in another Lanarkshire housing scheme in 1994, when ordinary law-abiding people banded together to protest at a wave of violence which had washed over their streets. But no one was given awards or medals by police and no one has, as yet, stood trial for the murder which sparked off the demonstrations.

In the early hours of Thursday, 25 August 1994, 21-year-old Douglas Bryce was gunned down near his home in Craigneuk, just outside Wishaw. He had been making his way home after watching the televised match between Rangers and AEK Athens with friends when someone pumped half a dozen bullets into him and left him for dead. The wounded man staggered across the road and collapsed in the garden of his parents' home.

Shortly afterwards, 28-year-old Alan Murdoch, who had been released from prison just 12 days earlier having served a sentence for the possession of a loaded firearm, was found knee-capped in his own car. The incident took place not far from where Mr Bryce had been murdered.

Mr Murdoch was just the latest in a long line of family members to be on the receiving end of a bullet or bomb. His brother, John, was shot in the back in December 1993, the bullet lodging in his spine and paralysing him from the neck down. A second bullet wedged in his knee. And another brother, William, was shot in the hand. Three men were charged with attempted murder but two of them were cleared because of a lack of corroborative evidence and the jury found the third Not Guilty.

After that, Alan Murdoch said he had kept the loaded automatic (which ultimately brought him his time in prison) nearby for his own protection. His home had already been the target of a gun attack the previous year, with bullets being sprayed through the bedroom window narrowly missing his wife and children. Later that same year, someone had lobbed a grenade at William Murdoch's house, shattering windows up and down the street. After the attack in his car, Alan Murdoch said he would be leaving the area because he was in no doubt that the people who had shot him would do the same again.

But it was the shooting of Douglas Bryce which enraged the town and prompted families, who had up until then kept their silence and their heads down, to take to the streets and give vent to their emotions. It started with the customary flowers and tributes left on the pavement where the man was shot. It developed into peaceful protest-marches against certain families in the area which, it was said, were feuding, fussing and fighting. It ended up in violence, as gangs of angry youths rampaged through the streets and stoned targeted houses.

Despite all this, the police investigation into the murder was stymied by a wall of silence. No one knew or admitted knowing anything about the slaying, which may have been the result of mistaken identity. But gradually, that wall crumbled and information began to trickle in until two men were arrested for the killing.

However, just days before their trial was scheduled to begin in the High Court of Glasgow in January 1995, they were released on the instructions of the Crown Office, who said the case against the men was not strong enough to proceed. Investigations were continuing, they said, but insiders felt it unlikely that sufficient new evidence would be found before the cut-off date for a trial, October 1995. (Under Scots Law an accused person who is to be tried on indictment for a serious crime, but who is out on bail awaiting trial, must be brought to trial within one year of his or her initial arrest.) At the time of writing, no such move has been announced.

Douglas Bryce's mother felt that the Crown Office was forgetting all about her son's murder. 'They are just shoving it to the side, until people forget,' she said bitterly. 'It is as if Douglas never existed. I don't think justice will ever be done in this case.'

Justice was certainly done in another case in which a man was gunned down in a city street by a killer said to be an underworld armourer. When police converged on the accused's home shortly after the shooting, they found an arms cache under some floor-boards and recovered two handguns, a double-barrelled shotgun, two single-barrelled rifles as well as ammunition, swords and a bayonet.

It started, as such things often do, with a simple argument in a pub. John Wilson, 25, and Robert Sim, 23, called into the Shielings Bar in Shettleston in the east end of Glasgow on 9 November 1990.

They had just left the rehearsals of an Orange flute-band and were not regulars at this particular pub. Somehow, they found themselves involved in a disagreement with other customers over a girl. Witnesses later said that the angry words seemed to be aimed at Sim, with Wilson apparently trying to calm things down. According to Sim, when they left at closing time there was a group of males standing outside the pub and they began shouting at them. It would seem the argument was far from over as far as John Wilson was concerned. Peacemaker or not, it would appear that he wanted to take it further.

At about one in the morning, four of the men who had been in the pub stood in a narrow bus shelter on Shettleston Road. Some of them were smoking cannabis. One of them heard a noise at the far entrance to the shelter and turned and saw John Wilson, a gun held in both hands and pointed in their direction.

'What do you want to say now?' he shouted and then fired. Andrew Ralston, aged 23, flattened himself against the glass window of the shelter as the gun went off and felt pain on the right side of his chest. Then, he said, he heard his friend, 24-year-old Stephen Barnes, making a gurgling noise. He began to tip forward and one of the other witnesses helped him out of the shelter, but he broke away from him and ran a few paces before collapsing; his head glancing off the side of a taxi as he fell.

Meanwhile, Wilson was standing in the same position, a trickle of smoke apparently drifting from the barrel of the pistol in his hands.

The single bullet had grazed Ralston's chest and punched clean through one of Barnes's lungs. The resulting internal bleeding literally choked the man to death. He was dead before the ambulance arrived.

Sim had stayed outside the shelter during the shooting. He did not know his friend had a pistol. He said Wilson had gone into the bus shelter, he heard a gun going off and saw a boy fall from the exit. He shouted at Wilson, 'You've shot somebody!' and Wilson merely replied, 'I know, I know.' Sim said he ran away and kept running for as long as he could. After that, he walked the streets in something of a daze before contacting his solicitor and together they walked into a police station where Sim gave himself up.

Police searched the bed-sit flats in which Wilson and Sim lived in Hamilton Road, Mount Vernon, and found the weapons hidden under the floorboards of a hall cupboard. Wilson subsequently pled guilty to the charge of reset regarding the arms. He was also found guilty of murdering Stephen Barnes and attempting to murder Andrew Ralston and was therefore sentenced to life in prison. As the judge handed down the sentence, Wilson smiled and shouted at the bench, 'I'll no sleep the night!'

His defiance did not end there. As he was led from the dock, he turned to the family of his victim who were seated in the public benches, and shouted 'Bang! Bang!' The Barnes family, outraged at this, began to scream at him, some straining forward to get at the convicted killer, and had to be held back by court officers, who eventually cleared the gallery. Sim had already been removed from the dock, having been found Not Proven of the murder and attempted murder.

Glasgow's criminal world has always been violent but in recent years it appears to have grown in savagery. In years gone by, the favoured weapons were generally bladed – the knife, the razor, the carpet-cutter. But, as has already been pointed out, the gun has become more and more prevalent. Since 1990 it seemed that every day brought news of a fresh shooting, as rival gangsters struggled for supremacy. Sometimes, the manner of the death suggested that the hoodlums had studied their fictional movie counterparts to gather pointers.

Men have been shot 'Mafia-style' in the back of the head as they sat in parked cars. Convicted drug-dealer Arthur Thomson Junior was shot in the street, the killer escaping in a fast car. Guns have been fired through windows and doors. Gang members have been wounded or killed as they sat at home with their families or while out having a quiet drink. Between 1992 and 1994 a casual dip into newspapers would have made the reader think the city was at war – as indeed some parts of it were. And still are. In the early part of 1995, the focus shifted to Renfrewshire, to the south-east of the city, where an alleged drug war apparently led to gunplay and death.

But not all gun-related crimes are committed by or against those with criminal leanings. Ordinary citizens – 'civilians' to the underworld – usually commit the most shocking acts, although generally there is some history of mental instability in the background.

Daphne Pertwee, for instance, had a long history of depression and suffered from a form of schizophrenia. Prior to her marriage to her husband, Roger, in 1982, she had been admitted to an institution in the south of England. After her release she had been receiving a course of injections. She had been advised by doctors not to have children, but she fell pregnant soon after she and her husband moved to Kincardine O'Neill in Deeside. The medication was halted to prevent any damage to the foetus.

But after the birth of their son, Henry, in December 1992, the 37-year-old woman's condition went downhill. She was admitted as a voluntary patient to Aberdeen's Royal Cornhill Hospital. She responded well to treatment, but at one point had to be given electro-convulsant therapy. In March 1992 she was allowed home, although medical treatment was to continue.

Five days after being released, on the evening of 25 March, she fed young Henry and placed him in his cot to sleep. Her husband had returned home shortly before and had gone to bed for a nap. Mrs Pertwee dined with some family friends, who said they had found her a touch distant, and at about 9.00 p.m. she told them she was going to check on the baby and her husband, who was still sleeping.

As the friends sat in the living-room, they heard two loud bangs from the bedroom and Mrs Pertwee walked back in and stated with chilling simplicity, 'I've just shot them both.' She had at no time prior to that said anything about her husband and child; she had not mentioned any arguments or disagreements – although it later emerged that their antique business had run up debts to the tune of £12,000 and this had caused some disharmony. After she announced what she had done, the woman sat down in the living-room to await calmly the arrival of the police. A police officer who arrived soon after said he found the woman to be 'vacant' but aware of what was happening.

Meanwhile, one of the visitors had run upstairs to the bedroom and found Roger Pertwee lying on his right side. The back of his head had been blown off. The four-month-old baby boy was also dead in his cot.

The woman said she did it because she suffered from severe depression and could not cope. A psychiatrist told the court that she posed a substantial risk to herself and to the public. She was later ordered to be detained in a psychiatric hospital without limit of time.

Meanwhile, in January 1991, a man described as 'cheery' and 'friendly' by neighbours took a shotgun and killed his wife, his two sons and himself. No one yet knows for sure why. The family – 26-year-old Gavin Simpson, his 20-year-old wife, Lorraine, and their sons Daniel, aged two, and Martin, aged nine months – were found dead in their Perthshire home by police.

But it took an almost casual act of terror, totally unconnected to any criminal activity, to really stir up the politicians and have them clamouring for stricter gun control.

GUN LAW

Like every other city, the pace of life in the centre of Glasgow changes throughout the day. During the daylight hours, the beat is dictated by commerce: office workers making their way to work, shoppers moving swiftly from store to store, the diesel roar and the hissing brakes of buses and taxis transporting more people into the mêlée.

At night, the rhythm changes. The shoppers in their comfortable shoes have left and the shuffling on the pavement transforms into the tap of high-heels as the city centre's new visitors seek out entertainment. There is a pulse in the air, underscored by the sound of music throbbing from open pub doors. The colour of night now glows with a neon intensity, sparkling down from cinema frontages, glittering from bar signs and windows, glinting from advertising hoardings.

It seems as if the city never rests. Even in the early hours of the morning, pleasure-seekers are moving from one place to another. Groups of young people, banished from licensed premises by the strictures of law but perhaps still in search of a friendly smile and a willing spirit, seek out a club or disco where the art of lifting and laying can still be practised.

Violence can erupt at any time during this period. Alcohol and drugs can enrage those shadowy areas of the human psyche which might normally lie dormant. Jealousy, envy, hate and anger can grow and envelop an individual until he or she erupts in sudden and occasionally horrific madness. Glasgow – to some the city of the blade but in reality generally no worse than anywhere else – saw an epidemic of seemingly random slashings and stabbings in its streets during 1992. In some of these incidents of bloodletting, drugs lay at the root.

But for too many others, bystanders caught up in a totally unprovoked situation outwith their control, a night out became a nightmare. One young man was murdered in a Sauchiehall Street club during 1993, apparently being stabbed to death in a toilet as he went to help someone whom he thought was being threatened by others. Two men were subsequently sentenced to life for his murder, although the complete truth of what happened in that small killing area has yet to be revealed.

That year, the authorities and police moved to stamp out the city-centre violence. A curfew was imposed on people who wanted to attend Glasgow's discos and clubs. The owners of these premises were not allowed to admit anyone after midnight. These proprietors, who said they were already upgrading their in-house security arrangements, complained bitterly about what they saw as draconian measures and were fearful of a sharp drop in profits. But their words fell on deaf ears. The measures appear to have worked, with the incidences of violence having been severely cut. Or perhaps the spate of slashings was merely some form of cycle, anyway, and with some of the knife-wielding thugs out of the way in prison, the figures naturally settled back down to normal levels.

The installation of close-circuit television in city streets has also, apparently, reduced levels of crime even further. Civil liberties activists, however, see their increased use as an infringement of rights while critics point out that the violence has merely moved to those areas not covered by the watchful camera lenses. Meanwhile, at the time of writing, there is talk of rescinding the curfew order.

The weapons of choice in these situations were always edged. Carpet, steak, fishing and kitchen knives were the preferred tools. Firearms are seldom, if ever, in evidence. However, they are certainly used with alarming regularity in areas of Glasgow where rival gangs continue to wage war over the drug and extortion trade. Guns are also used more and more in robberies. But the city centre, apart from one occasion, has remained mercifully free from the sound of gunfire.

But the event with which we are concerned had nothing to do with organised crime. It had nothing to do with drugs, or jealousy, or hate. The reasons behind the random shootings were known only to the young man who committed them.

And they died with him.

Alan Parkhill had two great passions in his life. One was his Land-Rover. The other was his shooting.

The 24-year-old man was an expert shot and what could be called a 'gun nut'. He owned a number of weapons, including a 9mm automatic pistol (the kind favoured by police forces and Ministry of Defence police), a .22 Colt revolver, a .45 Colt (the modern equivalent of the gun that won the West), .357 Smith & Wesson revolver, a .22 Winchester rifle, a .233 Remington hunting rifle and a .357 Magnum revolver – which is not quite the most powerful handgun in the world, but is still a potent weapon in anyone's hands. And Alan Parkhill was a crack shot.

Despite what some people might say was an unhealthy interest in firearms, Parkhill was not deemed a dangerous person. He was a mild-mannered young man who had been officially vetted by the police and cleared to own and use firearms. He had been authorised to own and use a shotgun since he was 16 and every one of his weapons was legally registered and correctly stored in his home within locked metal cabinets. A member of both the Balornock Rifle and Pistol Club and the Glasgow and District Pistol Club, he had also been given permission to acquire yet another .44 handgun. This home arsenal was later described as being 'normal for an average gun enthusiast'.

At one time he had even owned a semi-automatic weapon. However, he had quite properly surrendered this to police following the outlawing of such weapons in the wake of the Hungerford Massacre in 1987, when Michael Ryan ran amok with an AK47 and a pistol, gunning down 16 people before shooting himself. The ensuing political uproar forced the government to ban the semi-automatics and issued an order for all such weapons to be handed in. They offered little or no compensation to the owners and so only a fraction of those held legally were brought in. Rules regarding pump-action shotguns – which Ryan also owned but did not use on that dreadful day – were also strengthened.

The Hungerford incident prompted Parkhill to write a letter to the Shooting Rights Association – the British equivalent of America's National Rifle Association – which was, in his opinion, 'weathering the forthcoming storm' over the English shootings, saying that he realised it was now time to safeguard shooting in Britain and pledged his full support. But while he supported the rights of the shooting fraternity, he did deplore Ryan's actions. When discussing the shootings with a publican acquaintance, Parkhill said that anyone who did what Ryan had done should be 'hung, drawn and quartered'.

A blacksmith working for a Glasgow metal fabricators, Parkhill was described by his employer as a 'nice guy – quiet, reserved and a good ambassador for the company'. But in the early hours of 18 March 1990, this quiet, nice guy – as so many quiet, nice guys have done before and will no doubt do again – for some reason turned killer.

On Saturday, 17 March, he had attended a birthday party, where he was seen drinking Budweiser American lager. Later, he was also seen downing a further six pints of lager in a pub and, just before midnight in another pub, he added two gins and tonic. During this time he had appeared friendly and had not been arguing with anyone at all. As he left the last pub, he said to the owner that he could not remember where he had parked his Land-Rover. The publican suggested that he find a taxi to take him home. Parkhill did not heed the advice. Perhaps if he had, he and his victim would be alive today.

Something was apparently gnawing at Alan Parkhill that night, something that only he knew about out, whether real or imagined. He had returned home during the evening and had, in the words of an assistant procurator fiscal at the later inquiry, 'armed himself to the teeth'. Why? What had made this nice, quiet guy decide to go out into the streets with a gun?

Whatever it was, a psychiatrist later theorised, it was forcing him to make some kind of grand gesture. It may be that he did not intend to take the drastic course of action he ultimately did. It may be that he did not know exactly what he was going to do. But when he climbed back into his Land-Rover that night, with additional cans of beer under the driver's seat, a 9mm Browning automatic tucked in a shoulder holster and over twice the legal limit of alcohol in his bloodstream for driving, he started a countdown that would lead to two deaths.

At approximately 1.40 a.m. on Sunday, 18 March 1990, just as late-night revellers were making their way through the streets towards taxis or clubs, 20-year-old Tracy Patrick and her friend were waiting to cross the road at the junction of Renfield Street and Sauchiehall Street. They had just left the Savoy disco in Sauchiehall Street and were heading for a late-night bus to take them home.

As they finally moved across the road, Tracy's friend heard the Land-Rover careering towards them over the slight rise at the top of Renfield Street and managed to throw himself out of the way. Tracy, however, was not so quick. The vehicle slammed into her and sent her flying through the air. Thankfully, the blow did not kill her, although she did suffer a fractured arm and severe back injuries. Witnesses saw the driver slump forward in his seat, his head resting on the steering wheel. One said that she saw a crowd gather round the Land-Rover and had the impression that there was an ugly mood in the air.

Student Thomas McIntyre and his friends, Steven Devlin and Carmen Hannah, were making their way home from a dance in the College of Art – a Charles Rennie Mackintosh-designed building situated on a hill behind Sauchiehall Street. He saw the accident and leaped forward to help the injured girl. As the young man ran towards her, Alan Parkhill seemed to come to his senses and climbed out of the Land-Rover, pulling the Browning from the holster under his arm. He calmly crouched down in the classic pistol-shooter's pose, knees slightly bent, arms stretched in front of him, elbows crooked, the gun gripped in both hands, and aimed at the approaching Thomas McIntyre. And then he fired.

The first bullet caught Thomas McIntyre on the wrist. He spun round as the gunman fired another four bullets in quick succession, each one of them finding their mark – three clustered over the heart, the fourth burrowing into his back and bouncing around in his chest before erupting from his left arm. The young man, who had only been rushing to help an accident victim, died instantly.

Taxi-driver James Carlin had just deposited two passengers in Renfield Street and was going to move on to a nearby taxi rank just as the shooting began. He saw Tracy Patrick being struck by the Land-Rover and dispatched a message for help down his radio. He then left his taxi and was running towards the girl when he saw Thomas McIntyre turn and fall. The taxi-driver felt something hitting him on the stomach just below his belt. He later found out that he had been hit by a bullet which had passed right through the dead man. Luckily for him though, the bullet's velocity was almost spent and it did not break the skin, merely leaving a large red mark.

Meanwhile, Parkhill was firing indiscriminately at the crowds around him. People ducked for cover as bullets whined around them. They hid behind cars and in shop doorways, and crouched in the street praying none of the wild bullets would find them. Parkhill had fired at Tracy Patrick's friend as he tried to help her. The young man had looked up as the gunman was taking aim and threw himself to the side just in time. It was his second lucky escape that night.

But others were not so lucky. Steven Devlin was crouching over the injured girl when Parkhill shot him in the back and then again in the legs as he pitched over. Twenty-year-old Carmen Hannah was also seriously wounded in the leg when a bullet ploughed through her left calf and out the other side. She dragged herself into a shop entrance where bank clerk Christine Johnston and student nurse Christine Thomson were taking shelter. They had been making their way to a disco when the firing began. A stray bullet had lodged itself between Miss Thomson's boot and her foot, the resulting small wound later requiring four stitches. Her friend was hurt on the arm by two pieces of shrapnel.

Parkhill emptied 11 bullets from a 12-bullet magazine at the bystanders. He had killed one person and wounded five others. Who knows what he was thinking just at that instant. He had placed everything he loved in jeopardy. He had been driving while drunk, he had shot and killed who knew how many people. Perhaps he could see only one way out. Placing the Browning's muzzle to his right temple and with a final look at the world he had just turned upside down, he pulled the trigger. The bullet blasted through the front part of his brain and exploded out of the other side. His body crumpled and collapsed on to the road, the gun slipping from his nerveless fingers, clattering on to the concrete.

34

Police officers who arrived on the scene within seconds, found further live rounds lying beside him.

Ambulances rushed the injured people, including Parkhill, to Glasgow Royal Infirmary. Thomas McIntyre was dead on arrival while both Steven Devlin and Carmen Hannah were rushed into emergency surgery. They remained in a critical stage for several days, for although they had been treated for gunshot wounds, the shock to the system of such a wound can often be fatal. The other three wounded people were not seriously injured. Meanwhile, a nurse and a uniformed police officer who were removing Parkhill's jacket, found further ammunition and a sheath knife.

Witnesses to the shooting were taken to Stewart Street Police Office to give statements, while Renfield Street was blocked off by police to allow investigation teams to pore over the Land-Rover and the area immediately surrounding it. But although they knew what had happened, they did not know why. In the days and weeks that followed, detectives interviewed 200 people but came no closer to finding out what had motivated Parkhill.

A tight cordon was thrown around the home of the gunman's parents. They were not to blame for what their son had done, but often, some people do not see it that way. Angry mobs have the habit of gathering after events such as this and if they cannot take it out on the person responsible, then they will turn their blind hatred on the next best thing, his relatives. Members of the press also clamour round the homes of both the guilty person and the victim. At a later inquiry, the 52-year-old father of Thomas McIntyre said that reporters had besieged his house for days after the shooting.

Meanwhile, brain-dead but still breathing, Parkhill lay in a bed in the infirmary's intensive-care unit with police officers constantly at his side. They were hoping he would regain consciousness long enough to tell them why he had gone berserk. Some of them knew deep down that the young man would never come round again. They were correct. At 5.00 p.m. on Tuesday, 20 March, Alan Parkhill succumbed to his self-inflicted injury, taking the secret of his rampage to the grave.

Students at St Andrew's College in Milngavie, where Thomas McIntyre had been studying, held a special service in his memory and also prayed for the recovery of his friends Steven and Carmen.

35

Mr McIntyre, a former schools basketball champion, was described as a well-liked and hard-working student. He should have had everything ahead of him – a life, a career, a family. His life and his future were taken away from him in one moment of explosive madness. On Friday, 23 March, friends and family filled the Holy Faith Church in Mossend, Bellshill, for the popular student's funeral.

Predictably, Parkhill's gunshots echoed with calls for a tightening-up of gun laws. Just as predictably, there has since been a tinkering with the legislation but, some say, not nearly enough. Like all arguments, the right and wrong depends on which side of the trigger you stand. No one knows how many weapons there are in circulation, both illegally and legally. Of course, the vast majority of legitimate gun enthusiasts are respectable, level-headed people who adhere to all the rules regarding firearm ownership. Many of them do not shoot for the rather dubious pleasure of seeing fur and feathers flying, but are members of gun clubs where they blast the living daylights out of targets and clay pigeons. In an ideal world, if there were no guns then there would be no shootings, However, the number of crimes committed by properly licensed and registered firearms and shotguns are comparatively infinitesimal, while criminals with a mind to use a shooter will find one, no matter what.

The pro-shooting lobby point out that Britain enjoys a great deal of success at sporting events for shooting, largely due to people taking an interest in the sport at an early age. Those against shooting counter by saying heaven forbid that we might not win a few gold medals!

A more telling argument, though, is that any major ban could affect the economy of rural areas. Hunting brings over 50 million pounds into Scotland and is responsible for the creation of thousands of jobs. But feelings were strong among those Scots who do not hunt or shoot against firearms after the Parkhill shootings.

Labour MP for Clydesdale constituency Jimmy Hood said at the time, 'If the choice is between banning clubs or allowing them to continue as sources of weapons for criminals or mentally un-stable individuals, then the clubs should be banned.' Brian Wilson, then Labour's front-bench spokesman on Scottish affairs, echoed his fellow party member's remarks. Although he did not call for a complete ban of clubs, he did, however, criticise the measures taken for control of handguns. He said, 'This is another tragic case which calls into question the effectiveness of control over the possession of lethal weapons. The bottom line is that nobody should be able to walk about in public with one of these things, which have no legitimate purpose outwith the confines of a club.'

The Scottish Police Federation joined the argument, calling for an all-round clampdown on gun ownership. Ian Black, the Federation chairman, told the (then) *Glasgow Herald*, 'Once again, as at Hungerford, we have had someone shooting people he did not know and with whom he had no quarrel.

'If firearms are to be used only in gun clubs . . . then they will become the targets of terrorist organisations. If club members are allowed to take them home, those weapons become targets for casual theft and a potential danger to the public if anyone getting his hands on one goes off the rails.'

There had been 11 cases involving firearms in Strathclyde in the first three months of 1990. By American or even London standards this was a drop in the ocean, but it was a very real cause for concern in Scotland. In 1989, for instance, recorded cases of robbery in Scotland in which a firearm was used rose from the previous year's figure of 135 to 205 – 89 per cent of which took place in Strathclyde. However, it has to be pointed out that only five of those cases saw the weapon being discharged. In the same year, the number of cases where someone was injured after a weapon was fired dropped by nine per cent. By the first half of 1994, the gun-crime figures for Strathclyde rose to 360 cases – 60 per cent of the Scottish total – although in the country as a whole, the number of crimes and offences using firearms dropped by 9 per cent compared with 1992.

And so, it was in this emotional atmosphere that on Tuesday, 25 September 1990, the Fatal Accident Inquiry into the case began in Glasgow Sheriff Court. It would last six days.

A Fatal Accident Inquiry can be to Scotland what a Coroner's Inquest is in England, the only difference being that inquests are held as a matter of course south of the border, while in Scotland an FAI need only be held if the authorities deem it necessary. Obviously, they deemed it necessary in this case – but there are other instances where most right-thinking people felt some form of public investigation was called for, but denied.

The inquiry heard that Parkhill had owned a number of weapons and had held a shotgun licence from the age of 16 and had obtained a firearms certificate at 17. When police visited his home shortly after the shootings, they found his arsenal of weapons and a poster of Clint Eastwood as Dirty Harry. This was something the Crown emphasised during the inquiry, pointing out that one of his weapons was a .357 Magnum, similar to the model used by Eastwood when playing the San Francisco cop. Miss Elizabeth Munro, leading the evidence for the Crown, even said that Parkhill adopted 'a Clint Eastwood-like pose as he blazed away with an automatic pistol'.

However, Parkhill's father revealed that the poster was the only one they took from his son's bedroom and it seemed to him that they were trying to make Alan out to be 'something of a cowboy'. The police countered by saying they were only interested in items related to a shooting. In other words, if Parkhill had a poster preaching peace and light, then it was of no interest to them as it did not fit what they were looking into.

Glasgow psychiatrist Dr Raymond Antebi said that, faced with the loss of everything he loved by driving with more than twice the legal limit of alcohol in his bloodstream – Parkhill's blood count was 180 while the limit is 80 – the gunman may have decided to end it all in spectacular fashion while at the same time showing off what a superb marksman he was. He said that his possession of the Dirty Harry poster showed he had some identification with a hero figure. 'The position of his body when he was in the process of shooting would also indicate that he wanted to convey a dramatic performance,' he said. Perhaps – but the position Parkhill adopted was the classic marksman's stance, designed to aid accuracy and allow the user to compensate for the weapon's recoil.

The psychiatrist could only pose this as a theory, of course, as he had not been able to study Parkhill while alive and the young man had never previously shown signs of psychotic disorder. He said it was always possible that Parkhill had planned doing something all along that night. The fact that he was carrying a gun in a shoulder holster, as well as spare ammunition, suggested that he felt threatened by something or that he was under some form of pressure. Neither did he carry out the shooting in a frenzied manner – to work out that he had fired all but one of a clip, which he had saved for himself, showed some measure of calculation.

A solicitor for the Parkhill family argued that Alan Parkhill may have felt threatened by an angry crowd after he had hit the girl with his vehicle. He said it was as likely an explanation as that of the psychiatrist.

Elizabeth Munro thought differently, saying that there was no evidence of the crowd turning nasty, and even if they had 'stood frozen to the spot', she believed Parkhill would still have come out firing. She said that Parkhill had gone out drinking, gone home and 'armed himself to the teeth' and then gone out for some more drink. 'It was as if he was courting disaster,' she observed.

In a written judgment three weeks after the end of the inquiry, Sheriff Brian Lockhart returned a formal verdict, saying that neither the shootings nor the deaths could have been predicted, prevented or even explained. He also joined the gun controversy by calling for an examination of the gun control laws – particularly the age at which persons can legally obtain certificates – saying that the Firearms Consultative Committee (which was formed by Parliament after the Hungerford massacre) should pay attention to the issues raised by the Glasgow incident.

However, he did admit that it was difficult to say what change in the law would have prevented the Glasgow shooting, except the 'total prohibition of possession of firearms by any private individual'. To quote another gun-toting cinematic hero, 'That'll be the day.'

Cop Killers

ROAD KILL

ON THE MORNING of 28 July 1950, Constable 138D of the City of Glasgow Police made an unusual entry in the logbook of the police box in Cumberland Street in the Gorbals. The entry read:

> At 12.50 a.m. today a woman was knocked down and fatally injured in Prospecthill Road near Aikenhead Road. The motor car, believed to be a small, blue Austin, maybe 10hp, was driven by a man wearing a light-fawn Burberry coat. The car did not stop and was last seen driving eastwards in Aikenhead Road.

The logbook entry was unusual for two reasons. Firstly, this apparent hit-and-run would turn out to be the country's first murder by motor car. And secondly, the police officer who made the entry was himself the killer.

A little after midnight on 28 July 1950, taxi-driver John Kennedy came across the body of a woman lying in Prospecthill Road near the crest of a hill sloping towards the junction with Aikenhead Road, where the Divisional headquarters of F Division Strathclyde Police now stand. The woman was lying on her back, one leg folded across the other, her arms slightly outstretched at her sides. 'I thought perhaps she was drunk,' said Mr Kennedy later, 'or that she had been knocked down. Then I saw that her face was matted with blood.'

As the taxi-driver approached the body, a Glasgow Corporation maintenance lorry crested the brow of the hill and

41

came to a stop. Driver Samuel Murray and his partner, David Ashe, climbed out. Mr Murray had noticed a dark-coloured car with no lights on when they had passed that spot a short time before. Mr Ashe had commented that he thought he had seen a woman lying in the road behind the car but the lorry driver had merely assumed he was mistaken. As it turned out, he may have been the one who was wrong.

The woman's white shoes were lying some yards away from the body. She was wearing a red dress under a light coat. Fragments of her dental plate lay smashed on the roadway nearby. In the beam of their headlights, the three men could see black tyre tracks snaking up and over the body.

The police were called and Constable William Kevan was the first officer on the scene, arriving at 1.20 a.m. At first glance, it certainly looked as if the woman had been hit by a car which had then sped on. But Constable Kevan, working by torchlight, felt there was something more. With 23 years of police experience behind him, he had seen many a road accident and his instincts told him there was something not quite right about this whole set-up.

To begin with, he could find no broken glass in the vicinity. When someone is hit with some force by a car – and the severe injuries on the body certainly suggested that – there is often broken glass left twinkling on the road. Sometimes even a piece of the car, like a nut, screw, bolt or even a fender comes loose with the impact. But here there was nothing.

Professor John Glaister, the distinguished forensic pathologist who would play a pivotal role in the case, describes this as the theory of interchange. It is virtually impossible for a person to be present at a scene of a crime without either leaving something of himself or taking something of the scene with him. The most well-known example of this theory, also known as contact traces, are fingerprints, but it can also cover fibres of clothing, blood, hair, foot impressions, palm prints, mud, dirt, saliva and semen.

The theory can also extend to objects. The example given by Professor Glaister in his book *Final Diagnosis* (Hutchinson and Co, 1964) was that of a two-car collision. Each vehicle would be marked by the other, leaving scratches and dents which correspond with features on the other car and even fragments of paint. He said that this also applies when a car hits a human being – skin and clothing may carry traces of the vehicle, like the imprint of the radiator grille. The car will also bear the marks left by the body as it struck.

However, although there were no slivers of glass or other parts of the car left on Prospecthill Road that night, there was something left – the tyre tracks. And PC Kevan found them very interesting indeed. On looking closely, he could see that there were bits of flesh and spots of blood between the treads, which themselves converged to an apex, suggesting there was something wrong with one of the brakes. By examining these tyre marks carefully, Constable Kevan formed the opinion that they had been made by a car travelling first one direction and then the other. The marks began in a streaky fashion but became stronger where he surmised the car had stopped. There was another set of marks moving in the opposite direction. There was a set, he thought, for each time the car had driven over the woman's body, and it may have done so up to eight times.

PC Kevan contacted CID and informed them of his suspicions. He also said that he thought the car had been travelling at about 30 mph and that the dead woman had been laid down on the road prior to being run over.

If that was so, then this was definitely no hit-and-run.

It was murder.

The post mortem was carried out by Dr James Innis and Dr Andrew Allison. Dr Allison later said that the injuries on the body were 'more gross than I have ever met with in an accident due to a private car'. The doctors found that some of the injuries on the body had been made during life, underlining PC Kevan's theory that she had been incapacitated somehow and then laid down on the road and the car driven at her like an arrow at a target. One particular wound – on her right temple – was likely to have been produced by a blow from a blunt instrument.

However, although they believed that a car had been used as a weapon, the doctors were adamant that the woman had not been physically knocked down by one. When a person is hit by a speeding vehicle there are certain injuries that doctors expect to find, particularly on the legs. These injuries were not present in this case, although the torso, the pelvis and the face were badly mangled. It was their opinion that many of these injuries were caused after death.

43

Meanwhile, inquiries were being made to ascertain the dead woman's identity. The breakthrough came shortly after the body was discovered, when a woman reported her neighbour as missing, and it was only a matter of time before the police were able to confirm that the victim was 40-year-old, unmarried mother-of-two, Catherine McCluskey. She had worked in London for a time but had returned home to Glasgow at the height of the Blitz. At the time of her death, she was living a somewhat parlous existence in Nicholson Street in the Gorbals area of Glasgow.

It was in the Gorbals that she embarked on a relationship with a mystery man. Friends of the woman said she had often told them that she was seeing a policeman called John Robertson and that he was, in fact, the father of her youngest son, John, born on 22 April 1950. She told them that her lover was married and that she was receiving an allowance of nine shillings a week from him for the child. However, as police would later discover, Catherine had refused to identify the father of the child to the Public Assistance Office, the forerunner of the DSS, although she did admit to them that he was a police officer and that he was married. However, she told them that she was merely in the process of obtaining an allowance from him. At the time, she was in receipt of 33 shillings (£1.65) per week unemployment benefit and a supplemental allowance of eight shillings and sixpence (around 43 pence).

Elizabeth Coggan, her sister, said that Catherine had told her that 'the father could do nothing as he was a married man and that she had found out too late'.

The murder case was being investigated by Chief Inspector Donald MacDougall, an experienced officer known as 'Tiger' by criminal and policeman alike. What he had to ascertain as quickly as possible was if this police-officer boyfriend actually existed, or whether he was a figment of the dead woman's imagination. She lived, after all, in the Gorbals, at the time one of the darkest and toughest areas of the city and, as one commentator on the case suggested, there might be a certain advantage in a woman claiming a police officer as a paramour.

MacDougall already knew that Catherine McCluskey had supposedly been going to meet this man the night she was murdered – the friend who had raised the alarm had been looking after her children and became worried when she did not return. So, if he did exist, did she meet him?

Elizabeth Ross, a friend and neighbour, had actually seen Catherine talking to a policeman, whom she later identified as her boyfriend. Another, Rose O'Donnell, said she had seen Catherine in a dark-coloured Austin with a policeman three days before she died. The officer was deemed to be local and so inquiries were made at Oxford Street Police Station. Soon suspicion began to fall on one man, 33-year-old PC James Robertson.

A former aircraft-engine inspector, Robertson had been a police officer for five years with two commendations to his credit. The six-foot-one-inch-tall officer was handsome – with his black hair slicked back and neatly parted, and a razor-thin moustache cut sharply on his upper lip, he was the very image of the archetypal ladykiller. But he was a teetotaller and deeply religious, often attending meetings of the strict Plymouth Brethren. He was also married with two children. Could this be the man who had been having an affair with the dead woman, had knocked her cold and then calmly placed her behind his car before running the wheels over her?

Chief Inspector MacDougall learned that Robertson had been on duty the night before, but had been absent from his beat at the crucial time. PC Dugald Moffat told him that he had driven from Southern Division headquarters, then in Oxford Street, to their beats in the Gorbals in Robertson's Austin 16. At the muster before they left, they had been told that an Austin 16, registration number CVD 350, had been stolen in May from West Campbell Street near Bothwell Street and was still missing. Robertson parked the car as usual in a lane in Cumberland Street. What PC Moffat did not know at that point was that the Austin being driven by Robertson was the very same vehicle they had been told about at the muster, although Robertson had changed the registration number to DYS 570. At the time, though, Moffat and Robertson's other colleagues had no reason to suspect anything. Austin motor cars were, after all, very common – and Robertson was a police officer and therefore above suspicion. If you can't trust a policeman, who can you trust?

Fifteen minutes into their shift, Robertson announced that he had to leave his beat for a time. It was not uncommon for some officers to leave their duties to attend to personal business. Their friends were expected to cover for them should the need arise. Moffat, who was by now used to this from Robertson, asked him what he was going to do and Robertson replied, 'I'm taking a blonde home but I won't be as long as I was last night.' He then left in his car.

In 1950, Glasgow foot-patrol officers still used the police-box system to a great degree. Now probably more familiar to fans of *Doctor Who*, these boxes contained a telephone and logbook. Officers would also use them to store sandwiches and other personal items – on occasion alcohol – to help them get through a long cold night. When a crime had been committed and the officer was required to attend, the light on the top of the box flashed which he would see when next he or another beat-patrol officer passed. Glasgow police had been among the first forces in Britain to adopt the system in 1891 which was soon in use throughout the country. However, as radio began to become more common, the police boxes fell out of use. Most of them have been removed but there are two or three still to be seen gathering dust and billstickers in Glasgow streets. (At the time of writing, there is talk of converting one of these few remaining Glasgow boxes, in Royal Exchange Square, into a tourist-guide station.)

On this particular night, PC Moffat saw the light flashing on the Cumberland Street box. On answering the phone, he was told there was a disturbance in Cavendish Street. PC Moffat attended the locus where several people were duly arrested and taken to Oxford Street Police Station. There, the duty sergeant, Sergeant McAllister, asked Moffat where Robertson was and was informed that he had gone to the toilet. However, when the missing policeman did not show up, Sergeant McAllister and Moffat left the police station together to try and find him. In the street, they split up and at about ten past one in the morning, Moffat was relieved to see Robertson moving swiftly down Salisbury Street towards him. The out-of-breath officer told the sergeant that he had been trying to find them in the station but they had left without him.

Moffat noticed that Robertson's shirt collar was soaked with perspiration and when the man removed his hat there were thick sweat marks on the band. Robertson later told him that his car exhaust had broken off in Cathcart Road, saying that he had to stop and tie it up with a piece of rope, fastening the other end to a door handle. That explained the dirt Moffat could see on the man's trousers and shoes. Robertson commented that his car 'must've sounded like a Spitfire' and that he had noticed some people looking at him when it happened.

This was probably true. His exhaust had broken and he had possibly stopped in Cathcart Road to tie it up with the rope. What he did not say was that it had broken off when it had struck Catherine McCluskey's body as he reversed his car over her.

Robertson later told a similar story to another officer, PC John Dickson, who walked the next beat. Constable Dickson believed that the car belonged to a friend of Robertson's brother and that Robertson was looking after it while the man was out of the country.

Finally, after investigating for only one day, Chief Inspector MacDougall felt he had enough with which to confront the suspected man. He arranged with Sergeant McAllister to meet Robertson on his beat in Eglinton Street at about 1.45 a.m. on 29 July. When they approached him, the sergeant said: 'Is there any need to tell you who this is?'

'Oh no,' said Robertson, 'it is Mr MacDougall.'

Tiger MacDougall was a well-known figure on the force. Apart from that, like many another police officer and much to his embarrassment, he had even had a lift from Robertson in the stolen Austin 16. The detective told Robertson why he wanted to speak to him, cautioned him and then charged him with the murder of Catherine McCluskey.

'That, sir,' Robertson replied to the charge, 'is entirely wrong.' Later, when formally charged at the uniformed bar in the police station, he said, 'There is nothing more I can say. I have already replied to Mr MacDougall.'

Robertson was then searched and in the pocket of his trousers they found a rubber truncheon. The weapon was not standard police issue, although again it was not uncommon for officers to carry makeshift weapons with them for protection on the city streets. Bearing in mind that, according to the doctors, the dead woman had been struck on the temple prior to being laid in the road, the rubber truncheon was sent for examination. Forensic scientists later conducted a benzidine test for the presumption of blood on a stain found on the tip. However, the test could only show that the stain *may* have been blood since it was not sufficiently large for a more exact test to be made. (This test is no longer used by forensic scientists as the substance was found to be carcinogenic.)

Meanwhile, Chief Inspector MacDougall found the Austin 16 in a local garage and arranged for it to be taken away for forensic study. A search of Robertson's home unearthed two registration books and a key-ring carrying 18 car keys hidden in a tallboy. Police also found a wireless which had been stolen, along with a number of registration books, from the premises of Marine Motors, 147 Cumberland Street, on 23 April. Robertson denied committing the burglary, saying rather lamely he had found the radio and the books lying in a back court. Perhaps in his heart of hearts he knew that if a suspect had told him such a story, he would not have believed him either. He also denied stealing the car, claiming to have found it in Hillington Road. He said it had been sitting there for two days and he simply started it up and drove it away. After that, he changed the number plates – using a number registered to a tractor in Ayrshire – and passed the car off as his own.

The car itself was being scrutinised. The exhaust was indeed damaged. In fact, the silencer had broken away from the chassis, forcing it upwards towards the floorboards where it struck the pro-peller shaft. Police examiners believed that the silencer had made contact with a 'soft bodied' object which was then bounced towards the near rear wheel and then came out from under the car via the front wheel. Traces of blood were found on the underside and also what appeared to be hairs. On examination, some of these hairs were found to be 'closely similar' to the deceased but others were from an animal, probably a dog. Police examiners had also found pieces of flesh attached to the underside, while fibres which were discovered were similar to those taken from the dead woman's clothing.

It was at this stage that Professor Glaister became involved, studying the car in the yard of police headquarters. He experi-mented at great length with his own body and that of a police-woman volunteer who resembled Catherine McCluskey in size and build, recreating what may have happened in Prospecthill Road. He found one mark on the rear bumper of the car but he did not believe this had been caused by striking a human body. He read all the medical reports, learning that the only injuries on the dead woman's legs were on the inside of the knees – and not on the front or back of the legs as he would expect if she had been knocked down. When he looked at prepared slides of tissue from these wounds, he was certain they had been caused after death.

So the scenario presented by the police and scientific evidence was this: Robertson had taken the woman in his car to Prospecthill Road. There he had somehow incapacitated her, possibly by striking her with the rubber truncheon. He had then placed the unconscious body in the road, laying it parallel to the car's wheels, reversed the car over her, stopped a few yards down the road and then driven over her again, then reversed back again and driven forward again, possibly up to eight times.

But while they were working all this out, Robertson was giving his solicitor a different picture of events. At first, Robertson denied everything, but his solicitor, Laurence Dowdall, was a good friend of Tiger MacDougall and from him he learned much of what was against his client. At a second meeting his client conceded that he had known Catherine McCluskey. In fact, he confirmed that they had been romantically involved. His version of what happened on that dark night was plausible but, given the weight of scientific evidence and expert opinion against it, might be seen in hindsight as being doomed to failure. However, one expert's opinion could be refuted by another and both the solicitor and defence advocate Mr John Cameron, KC (later Lord Cameron) agreed that if Robertson was honest about his involvement with the dead woman then he might at least escape the gallows. Robertson agreed to do as they recommended. At first.

The trial began on Monday, 6 November 1950, in the High Court of Glasgow, a magnificently porticoed building on the Saltmarket, facing Glasgow Green and the square where the public gallows once stood. The case was a local cause célèbre and queues for the public gallery began to form at 7.30 a.m. – two and half hours before the doors opened. Every seat in the gallery was eventually filled while other people waited outside for people to leave so that they could take their place. Some of them had come prepared, carrying with them flasks of tea and packets of sandwiches.

Whatever happened, the trial had to be concluded by Wednesday, 16 November. Under the Scottish Criminal Procedures

Act, an accused person being held on remand had to have his trial concluded within 110 days of his arrest – a period which ended on that day. (These rules have now changed so that a trial need only begin before the 110 day cut-off.) As it turned out, the trial took only a week. Prosecution had 80 witnesses to call, defence only three – and two of them were expert witnesses.

Throughout all the evidence, Robertson sat impassively in the dock, listening to his defence counsel trying to poke holes in the prosecution's insistence that this was a deliberate act of murder; that he had killed Catherine McCluskey because she had become a danger to his marriage. They prised at the opinions of police officers and medical men who maintained that the dead woman had been placed behind the car, trying to get them to concede that it was possible that a car reversing down the hill could have knocked the woman off her feet and under the car.

Professor Glaister was asked about the flesh which had been torn from the woman's knees. The professor pointed out, 'You will find the injuries are not on the knees. They are on the inner aspects of the knees and my experience of the female anatomy is that a woman does not stand presenting that part to an oncoming car.' Roberton's KC jumped on the evidence of the small dent on the bumper, asking Professor Glaister, 'So far as the motor car is concerned, there is evidence on the rear which is at least consistent with collision between the car in reverse and a human body?'

'Among other things,' replied the professor.

Mr Cameron pressed, 'But it is at least consistent with a human body?'

'That is one of a vast collection that could not be eliminated.'

'You cannot eliminate it?'

'No.'

But the KC was unable to shake the various witnesses' opinions that Catherine McCluskey was not knocked down by the car but was laid down in a parallel position to the car's wheels and deliberately run over more than once. However, the defence did produce their own expert witnesses to say that it was possible that the death was accidental.

They were doing a good job on Robertson's behalf. They had, it would seem, managed to undermine a certain amount of the Crown's case against their client, possibly placing more than a shadow of a reasonable doubt in the jury's mind. Although some witnesses had identified Robertson at an identification parade as the police officer they had seen with Catherine McCluskey, one of them failed to point him out in court, pointing instead at a journalist – this despite the fact that identification in court is something of a joke considering the accused is sitting isolated in the dock with two smartly uniformed police officers at each side. Mr Cameron also showed, using Mr Dowdall as a model, that it was virtually impossible for a man sitting in the driving seat of a car to stun a passenger with the rubber hose held in his right hand.

By the fifth day of the trial, the defence were confident, if not of an acquittal, then at least of a guilty verdict on a lesser charge. But then Robertson took the stand and, against the advice of his legal representatives, denied that there had ever been a relationship between him and Catherine McCluskey. He had warned his solicitor of his decision just prior to taking the stand, telling them he felt he could not embarrass his wife and family in public by admitting to an infidelity. Laurence Dowdall tried to convince him otherwise but the accused man was adamant. He was going to bluff it out. He was confident.

In the witness box, he claimed his acquaintanceship with Catherine McCluskey was merely a passing one. He told the court he had met her when he attended a disturbance in Nicholson Street, where she lived. He had driven the woman and her children home on one occasion, but he had never been in her home.

He admitted he had told Constable Moffat that he was going away for a few minutes to meet a blonde but insisted that it was a turn of phrase. Actually, there may be something in this – Catherine McCluskey was dark-headed. She had asked to meet him, he explained, because she was going to be evicted from her house for non-payment of rent. She asked him to drive her out to a friend's house in Neilston where she might be able to arrange alternative accommodation. Robertson said he tried to explain to her that he could not drive her to Neilston and she started to weep. He took her for a run in the car, driving via Pollokshaws Road and Cathcart Road to a lonely and dark section of Prospecthill Road. Catherine asked him then to drive her to Rutherglen at least, but again he refused. He turned the car so that it was facing westwards on the road and told her he was going back to his duties.

'I said if she was going, she could go,' he told the court, his voice so hushed people had to lean forward to hear the words, 'but I was not waiting there any longer. I opened the door and she eventually got out.' He said that she appeared to find the situation funny. 'I told her that I was going back to Cumberland Street but if she insisted on standing there she would be left. At that time the car door was open. I shut the door. She was standing on the pavement on the south side of the road.'

He started the car, pushed it into gear and drove about 100 yards down the road, thinking, he said, that she would change her mind. Then he stopped and decided he'd better go back for her.

'It was very dark and there are no streetlamps there,' he said. 'I reversed back to where I thought she was. I was on the crown of the road most of the time and gradually steered the car to the pavement.'

The first thing he noticed was the tone of the engine growing louder. He said he felt 'a bit of a jar' but thought that could have been caused by the sudden deceleration as he stopped. He looked around but could not see Catherine. Then he opened the offside front door and started to get out. That was when he found her, he claimed.

'I saw her face on the ground below the offside running-board, immediately behind the offside front tyre. I knelt down. It was Catherine McCluskey.' His voice now scarcely above a whisper, Robertson said that her face was slightly to the side and he turned it over. Blood was bubbling from her mouth but, as he watched, it stopped and appeared to be sucked back in. He was certain she was dead.

He climbed out of the car, stepping over her face, and checked underneath. Her body and clothing appeared to be caught up on the propeller shaft. He tried to free her but was unable to do so. By this time, he said, he was panic stricken. He realised he was driving a stolen car, was absent from his beat and now had knocked a woman down. That was when he switched off the car headlamps. He contemplated jacking the car up and freeing the body that way, but he reasoned that the car's built-in jacks would only clear about an inch and that would not make much difference. Perhaps, he reasoned, if he drove the car forward a bit, that would help. He climbed back in and drove forward about a car length but this did no good, so he reversed again for another car length. This still did not release the body. Finally, he drove forward again and this must have done the trick because he was able to drive away. As he drove, he noticed that his exhaust was making a great deal of noise so he stopped again and tied it up, using the door handle as support.

The accused man's counsel looked him straight in the eye and asked, 'On 28 July 1950, did you assault Catherine McCluskey?'

'I did not!'

'Did you strike her on the head with a rubber truncheon!'

'No, sir.'

'Did you do anything to render her unconscious?'

'No, sir.'

'Did you deliberately drive a motor car over her and murder her?'

'No, sir. I did not.'

It was a bravura performance and one that may well have worked had he told the truth about his relationship with the dead woman. But in the end, his decision to lie to the court about the true nature of his relationship with the murdered woman may well have proved to be his undoing. The jury was out for one hour and three minutes and when they filed back into court they found him guilty of the theft of the car, the wireless and the registration books. The verdict was unanimous. As he listened to their finding, Robertson sat in the dock, his gaze fixed firmly on a point just below the judge's bench. Then the jury reached their decision on the most important charge, that of murder.

They found him Guilty. By a majority.

Only then did Robertson move and it was only to turn round slightly to his right and gaze coldly at the jury. He must have seen one of the woman jurors crying. He must have been thinking something but we will never know what. Then his gaze swivelled back to the judge as he pronounced sentence. Robertson stood as the judge placed the black cap on his head and told him that he would be taken from his cell and hanged. Then Robertson was led from the court.

Outside, word of the verdict reached the crowds in the Saltmarket. They pushed and jostled their way to the side of the building for a look at the police officer who had turned killer but the prison escort had erected a piece of tarpaulin to prevent anyone

A TIME TO KILL

seeing him as he stepped into the van which would take him to Glasgow's Barlinnie Prison.

There, Robertson took up temporary residence in the condemned cell. He launched an appeal which was refused. He made a plea for clemency. He had hopes of a reprieve of the death penalty right up until the final moments, but none came. On 16 December 1950 he was taken from his cell and led to the special gallows-room in Barlinnie, where the legal murder on behalf of society took place. By this time he was a pitiful sight, a shadow of the handsome and smartly turned-out man he once was. He had lost weight and his face had a sallow, hunted look.

Meanwhile, his wife broke her silence, telling the press that it was 'absolutely ridiculous' that her husband had led a double life. 'The facts are that my husband never went out himself,' she said. 'He was keen on his hobbies, gardening and carpentry, and when he went out he took us all with him, and at times the children only.'

But she was wrong. He *had* been having an affair with Catherine McCluskey and, if the prosecution were correct, had decided to break the hold she had on him by killing her. In the end, he could, apparently, bring himself to kill, but not to admit the affair. Laurence Dowdall later said Robertson was 'the fellow who chose to hang rather than let his wife down in public'.

The case of James Robertson, a police officer who killed, is unique in Scotland, although there is what could be seen as a similar case in Yorkshire.

On Good Friday 1994, 32-year-old Angela Jenkinson was found strangled on waste ground only 100 yards from her Bradford home. At the time of her death, Miss Jenkinson was seven months pregnant. The child died with her.

Nine hours after her body was found, Detective Constable Vincent Hand was arrested for her murder. He had apparently known the dead woman for eight years, first as an informant and then as a lover. The problem was, DC Hand was married, to another officer who was part of Bradford's Vice Squad.

According to the prosecution at one of DC Hand's 12 court hearings, the dead woman had been placing pressure on DC Hand regarding the baby, which she claimed was his, threatening to inform the Child Support Agency that he was the father. DC Hand,

54

they claimed, killed her while he was on surveillance duties near her home.

Whatever happened, the full story never came out in court. In September 1994, DC Hand disappeared while out on bail. The search for him concentrated on the Yorkshire Dales and the Lake District. But the accused officer had fled south, finally stopping in some remote woodland near the village of Melton Constable in Norfolk. There he ran a hosepipe from the exhaust pipe of his red Fiat Panda and filled the interior with fumes. His dead body was found two days after he had disappeared from Bradford.

The dead woman's family told reporters they believed the suicide was an admission of guilt, that the detective constable could not live with what he had done. But we will never know the complete truth.

Naturally, there have been other cases in Scotland where police officers – and former officers – have been convicted of wrong-doings, from theft to murder. For instance, in September 1994, a police officer with Central Scotland Police was jailed for a year after being convicted of fondling five girls aged 11 to 14 years over a three-year period. And in the same month, a former officer with the same force took full responsibility for attempting to smuggle one million pounds worth of hashish into Scotland from Morocco. The man, along with yet another former Central Police officer and a third man, went on trial in Melilla on the North Coast of Africa.

In March 1994, a Thurso police officer was sentenced to 18 months for perverting the course of justice. He had taken a pair of boots belonging to a man suspected of car theft and rubbed them in the glass from the smashed window of the car, which had over-turned, and also wedged a sliver of glass into a heel. This had been done after a colleague suggested that the suspect's footwear be submitted for forensic examination and the officer had said some-thing about 'making sure' there was glass on the man's boots.

On a similar theme, in February 1994, a sheriff claimed that two Lothian and Borders officers had rehearsed their evidence during a trial of a colleague, charged with breach of the peace.

In January 1973, three Aberdeen officers were disciplined for apparently terrorising a housebreaker by placing him naked beside a corpse in a mortuary. One of the officers was subsequently dismissed from the force while the other two were asked to resign. The Chief Constable of the day was criticised for holding the resulting inquiry in private, while press coverage of the affair also came in for censure.

But a policeman's lot can be a dangerous one. In 1969, former Glasgow policeman Howard Wilson teamed up with another one-time officer and a former prison officer to carry out two daring bank robberies. After the second raid, suspicious police officers who had called at Wilson's flat in Allison Street on Glasgow's southside were surprised when he turned on them with a pistol. Wilson killed two of them and seriously injured a third. He was subsequently sentenced to life imprisonment. While in prison he was involved in a much-publicised riot in Inverness Prison, but in recent years has settled himself into prison routine and even written a bulky thriller which was published in 1994. But 25 years after his conviction, he can still excite controversy. When it was revealed in 1994 that he may be released from prison soon, news-papers were filled with letters and quotes from police and public deploring the suggestion.

Other police officers have lost their lives in the course of duty. In April 1921, Inspector Robert Johnson was gunned down by IRA sympathisers as he travelled in a prison van carrying Frank Carty, a commandant in the IRA, to Barlinnie Prison in Glasgow. Detective Sergeant George Stirton was wounded in the rescue attempt. (For fuller details of this and the Howard Wilson cases, see *Blood on the Thistle*, Mainstream, 1992.)

In 1946, again in Glasgow, a former detective sergeant, James Straiton, was shot during a housebreaking in Dennistoun. A single fingerprint led police to 26-year-old John Caldwell, who was arrested, convicted and hanged on 10 August 1946.

And in 1952, 17-year-old Edwin Finlayson, being pursued for embezzling £1,200 from the bank where he worked, shot and killed Constable John McLeod and wounded Constable Thomas McDonald in Hyndland Road, in the west-end of Glasgow. Finlayson then ran into nearby Westbourne Gardens Lane where he shot himself as other officers closed in. They say his ghost still haunts the spot where he put the gun to his head.

In January 1979, three men were found guilty of murdering Glasgow butcher Thomas Woods, and attempting to murder his friend, Constable Brian Coppins, during a robbery. The hunt involved detectives not just in Glasgow, but also London and Amsterdam.

All of these cases underline just how dangerous a policeman's life can be, for whereas it is certainly true that there is a great deal of routine attached to their duties, it is also true that they can never know what they will meet around the next corner. A seemingly routine domestic dispute can suddenly turn violent – as happened in 1994 when officers in Glasgow responded to a call from a family about their son, a diagnosed schizophrenic.

The boy, 18-year-old Philip McFadden, had shown the first signs of schizophrenia at the age of 14, when he changed from a bright, well-behaved young boy into a sullen, uncommunicative youth who would spend long periods of time on his own or speaking nonsense. After treatment as a voluntary in-patient at the city's Gartnavel Royal Hospital, Philip's condition appeared to stabilise until, at the age of 16, he was allowed to live at home with his family, although still under treatment as an out-patient. He continued to take medication and received regular medical treatment in the hospital and at home.

Eventually, towards the end of 1993, he decided he was no longer going to accept treatment. He said he was feeling better and did not need it, although the death of his brother in an accident did affect him deeply. He also blamed himself for a fire in the family home in Kinning Park which forced them to move temporarily to a flat in the Gorbals. He stopped taking his medication and visits from a nurse ceased.

It was in the Gorbals flat that his condition deteriorated until, on 17 June 1994, his mother grew so concerned that she tried – in vain as it turned out – to obtain medical assistance. He had not received medication for four months. He had not slept at all the night before and was hallucinating, believing that one of his brothers had cut off his hand and had scarred his body with a knife. Neither claim was true. He then began to brandish a bread knife he had taken from the family kitchen. And so began a chain of events which would result in the death of a young police officer.

Alarmed and unable to get the knife off him, Mrs McFadden tried to obtain medical help. None was forthcoming, despite making as many as nine calls, she later said. Finally, a medical receptionist said that she would send a doctor and contact the police to provide him with an escort. But the family did not want the police involved, feeling that would be the worst thing possible for Philip at that time. They wanted medical help, not police help. If a doctor would come and treat Philip, the family were sure he would take his medication. A police presence, they felt, would only make things worse. But Mrs McFadden was told that a doctor would not come out without police protection. Meanwhile, Philip McFadden was turning his unstable attentions to his sister and accusing her of trying to kill him.

As time went on, and with still no sign of improvement in her son, Mrs McFadden took a taxi from her Gorbals home to her doctor's surgery to try and get some action. While she was away, the police arrived. Philip told them he needed the knife to protect himself. Also present at this time were his older sisters, Helena and Mary. The police officers told them to leave the house and go into the police van, which they did.

After that, Philip's schizophrenic episode appeared to worsen. As his feelings of paranoia deepened with the presence of the uniforms, the danger of violence grew. Eventually, it all became too much for his disturbed mind and he lashed out, threatening to stab four officers; chasing a sergeant in the street and trying to stab him – striking him on the arm; and finally murdering another constable, 28-year-old PC Lewis Fulton, by stabbing him on the head and body before eventually being caught and restrained.

The death of this likeable young officer shocked the city. Perhaps predictably, there were calls from some officers for the police force to be armed – or at least be given some form of protection other than a police-issue baton and a firm manner. An American police force sent Strathclyde a supply of knife-resistant body armour. They are also being armed, to the chagrin of Civil Liberties activists, with new side-handled and extendable batons which should help them keep a knife-wielding assailant at bay. These new batons are much more potent weapons which, in experienced hands, could break a bone as easily as snapping a twig. Critics feel it will merely bring an increase in the number of allegations of assaults by police officers, and they point out that the number of assaults on police in Strathclyde are actually falling, although police sources claim that an officer is assaulted every 174 minutes. However, the definition of police assault can be very wide indeed, ranging from spitting or shoving to a full-blown attack with a weapon.

At first, feeling against Philip McFadden was strong, with normally level-headed people even saying that he should have been shot in the street by a police marksman, as would have happened in America. However, as it became clear that Philip McFadden was insane and unfit to plead, and the facts of his mother's vain attempts to obtain medical assistance became known, even the Strathclyde Branch of the Scottish Police Federation launched a much-needed attack on the Government's controversial 'Care in the Community' policy.

Thomas Rowatt, the organisation's deputy general secretary, said that there was deep frustration and anger over the young officer's death. 'I am seriously concerned about the Government's commitment to care in the community,' he told *The Herald*. 'Obviously, Philip McFadden did not become insane overnight.

'If there was provision for him to get psychiatric care and it was being neglected, that is unacceptable, and it should be investigated. The police service has, sadly, become a dustbin, sweeping up the mentally ill whom the community is not looking after.'

Clearly, the McFadden family had not received enough advice on how to help their son through a schizophrenic episode. There had not been sufficient checks made to ensure that he was taking the medication to keep his condition in check. And the police force is not the body to deal with the mentally ill. They can provide protection and support to the professionals if need be, but officers are not trained in the best way to deal with an unstable personality.

And so, a young man who should have been receiving close and personal medical attention was placed in the State Hospital at Carstairs for an indefinite period of time. A family had to come to terms with the fact that their son and brother had been labelled a mad-dog killer, and the young wife and family of the dead officer faced the future without a husband and father. It is a tragedy that could occur again, as long as there is a government which puts balancing the books ahead of taking care of its less-fortunate people.

In August 1994, an official inquiry was made into murders committed by mentally ill persons who had been returned to the community. The report – Confidential Inquiry into Homicides and Suicides by Mentally Ill People – was requested by the Government following the death of an 11-year-old girl in a Doncaster shopping centre at the hands of a newly discharged psychiatric patient. The inquiry studied 22 cases which occurred between July 1992 and December 1993 and found that 13 of them involved a fall-off in attendance at treatment centres or a failure in some regard to take medication.

But the Government's response to the report was that it showed that it was 'extremely rare' for a mentally ill person to kill while in contact with specialist psychiatric services. Opposition speakers in return accused the Government of 'breathtaking complacency' over the subject. Political games were being played with lives.

Even a judge entered the controversy in February 1995, when he issued a summons against Health Secretary Virginia Bottomley, calling her to court to explain why a defendant who had been described in his court as 'very disturbed' could not receive a psychiatric bed.

Sharon Towes had pled guilty in Chichester Crown Court to malicious wounding after she attacked a council worker with a knife. She had appeared before Judge Anthony Thorpe seven times and on each occasion the judge had asked for her to be sent to a medium secure unit for treatment. Instead, she was sent back each time to Holloway Prison. Psychiatrists had stated that in their opinion, Miss Towes was 'an extremely dangerous young woman'.

The judge said he found this state of affairs 'unacceptable' in a 'modern, humane society' and ordered that, unless a bed was found within a day, he would issue a summons for the Health Secretary to appear before him and explain 'this sorry state of affairs'. The summons was set aside just over a week later and no politician was required to appear in court.

But back in Glasgow in 1994, in memory of the dead officer, Strathclyde Police placed a commemorative plaque in the foyer of Stewart Street Police Station – but a metal plate cannot replace flesh and blood. In addition, in February 1995, the Police Federation announced that they would be funding a memorial scholarship in Lewis Fulton's name at Glasgow's Caledonian University. The funding, estimated at between £3,000 and £4,000 per year, will allow a serving Strathclyde police officer to study for a masters degree or doctorate at the city's newest university. In March 1995, the Federation also threw their considerable weight behind calls for a Fatal Accident Inquiry into Constable Fulton's death.

And in September 1994, a CID officer from London embarked on a personal crusade to have police officers properly protected. Detective Constable Norman Brennan, a member of the Metropolitan Police's Robbery Squad in North London, said that he was 'sick and tired of police officers being murdered at such an alarming rate'. He continued, 'I think the hierarchy in the police and the police unions are out of touch with the men on the front-line. My aim is to wake up some people who seem to have been asleep for far too long and get some action.'

DC Brennan, who had been attacked 16 times and almost killed twice during his 16-year career, wanted the police to be armed and properly protected by the courts.

But arming the police is not the answer. The police believe that as soon as a criminal goes out armed with a gun, sooner or later that gun will go off. The same can be said of armed police. At present, only certain officers can be issued with firearms. They are selected, presumably, because of their ability to handle the weapon, both physically and psychologically. Some people should not be issued with weapons at all because they do not have the mental constitution to cope with the power they have at their hip or in their hand. There are officers who go over the top during an arrest, using their baton indiscriminately on the head rather than on the body as they are trained to do. Give these officers a more powerful weapon and there is always the possibility that they will use it just as badly if their temper flares or their judgment is weakened by anger, hate or just plain stupidity – one of the reasons the spread of the new-style baton is viewed by its critics with distaste.

On the other hand, there are more firearms in circulation in Britain's cities. But many officers believe that arming the police would make them more of a legitimate target to gun-crazy criminals; while criminals say that more of them would start carrying guns if the police were armed. The words 'vicious' and 'circle' come to mind.

It is still a comparative rarity for a Scottish police officer to be killed on duty. It is more common for civilians to be murdered indiscriminately or during a robbery, yet no one is suggesting that we should all walk about armed to the teeth.

When DC Brennan brought his message to Scotland following the death of PC Fulton, he visited Stewart Street Police Station where the officer had been based. He also went to Lanarkshire, to Larkhall, where another officer stabbed during the line of duty had been stationed. The case is another example of how a routine arrest can go horribly and tragically wrong . . .

THE BATTLE OF EARN GARDENS

When mine-owners brought Irish workers to Lanarkshire during the nineteenth century to act as scab labour against striking local workers, they were motivated solely by the pursuit of profit. For although the importation of cheap labour from a country ravaged by poverty and famine did manage to break the strikes and bring the Scottish miners to heel for a time, the rich owners had no idea that their actions would also result in spawning bitter hatreds that have lasted to this day. Their actions could also be viewed today as the closing of a circle – in the final years of the sixteenth century, King James VI of Scotland (and later James I of Great Britain) transplanted Scottish and English Protestants in Ulster, settling them in lands confiscated from the Catholic McDonnels of Antrim. His idea was to drive a wedge between the Scottish MacDonalds, who were defying Crown authority, and the Irish clan to which they were linked by marriage and tradition. No sooner had the Protestants landed on the Emerald Isle when they began to make their presence felt among the indigenous Catholics, helping to lay the groundwork for the troubles ahead.

Many of the families the mine-owners brought back to Scotland in the nineteenth century were part of the Orange Order, formed in troubled Ulster the century before. And they brought their hatred of Catholicism with them.

Of course, there had been religious troubles in Scotland before then – the Covenanters, for example – but the hatred of Protestants for Catholics (and vice versa), which has been passed on from generation to generation by some families in certain areas of

Scotland, dates back largely to the immigration of those Irish workers in the mid-1800s.

In Glasgow, you still find pubs which are either Orange or Republican; Rangers or Celtic, depending on how political or sporting your drinking views are. Until comparatively recently, certain areas of Glasgow were either Catholic or Protestant strongholds, a situation which changed as the face of the city changed, when neighbourhoods were ripped apart by town planners. And although the city and the rest of Scotland were generally not targets for Republican or Loyalist bombers – although three Glasgow pubs did suffer bomb attacks from locally based UVF members in 1979 – Scottish houses have acted regularly as arsenals or bomb-making factories. It is also said that some notable underworld figures in Glasgow's east-end are officers in one terrorist army or another, raising cash for the cause through criminal enterprises. In 1979, while 11 men were on trial for the aforementioned pub bombings, another nine were charged with conspiring to further the aims of the UDA in the city through fundraising and arms gathering.

But even today in Lanarkshire, the huge county which sprawls from the south-eastern edges of the city to the Border country, there are whole towns which swear allegiance to one side or another. Carfin, for instance, with its Grotto, is largely Roman Catholic, while Larkhall is Protestant.

There is a story which tells how the latter had the railings of the local park painted red, white and blue to commemorate the coronation of Queen Elizabeth. When council workers turned up to repaint them maroon, local residents banded together to insist that the loyalist colours be replaced, raising a 1,000 signature petition to back up their demand. Maroon, they said, was simply not appropriate.

The bitterness between the religions is not as prevalent now as it once was. But now and again it can flare up, usually round about the anniversary of the Battle of the Boyne on 1 July 1690, when the loyalist forces of King William (the Orange hero King Billy) fought and won what was little more than a skirmish with the retreating forces of the Jacobite (and Roman Catholic) James II at the River Boyne in Ireland. Around that date, in parts of Scotland and Ireland, members of the Orange Walk march and swagger through the streets to the sound of drum and flute bands, much to the annoyance of some Roman Catholics. It has been said that wherever there is an Orange Walk, trouble is not far behind – although there have not been any major disturbances of that type in Scotland for years, perhaps another sign that the strength of sectarianism is receding.

But now and again, underlying hatreds can rise to the surface and lead to tragedy. Early in the morning of Sunday, 5 June 1983, that was exactly what happened in Larkhall. It started off simply enough with an argument between two youths at a disco. It would end with one man dead and a normally law-abiding family ripped apart by a knife blade.

At the centre of all the trouble was Hugh Murray, then 16 years of age. He had found himself involved in a fight in the town with Alexander Matusavage and William Strang, both 17 years of age. During the fight, the epithets 'Fenian bastard' and 'Orange bastard' could be heard and, obviously, religious difficulties were somewhere at the back of it.

The disagreement began in the disco, where Murray apparently pushed Matusavage to the ground. This led to a full-blown fight outside, during which Matusavage said Murray went for him with a knife, stabbing him in the back, front and neck. 'All I can remember is my blood flowing down the pavement,' he said later.

His friend, William Strang, said he managed to push Matusavage away, then turned and saw Murray standing there with a knife in his hand. 'He jumped on top of Matusavage,' he said, 'and began ripping his back with the knife.'

Strang said he thought Murray intended to kill his friend and stepped forward to help, but stopped again when Murray whirled on him, snarling, 'If you grass me, I'll blade you.' But Strang went forward anyway, grabbing the knife in Murray's hand, his hand slicing open on the blade.

When Murray had retreated, the police were called and three CID officers – Acting Detective Constable Duncan Nicolson and Detective Constables John Hair and Wilson Gillan – were detailed to go to Murray's address and pick him up. Detective Sergeant Ross Hunt, based in Larkhall, had intended to go to Law Hospital where the two injured youths were being treated. DS Hunt knew Larkhall well – it was his home as well as his place of work – so he agreed to go along with them to 'hoover' up young Hughie. It was a fatal decision.

The four officers went to Earn Gardens, part of a council estate where Murray lived with his family. The street itself is a cul-de-sac. When they hammered at the door at about 2.00 a.m. on Sunday, 5 June, the wanted youth's mother, Jean, answered. They explained that they were looking for 'young Hughie' but Mrs Murray refused to let the police in – according to one witness staying in the house at the time this was because they did not have a warrant – and closed the door on them. The detectives decided to wait outside until Hugh returned.

They did not wait long. A short time later, they saw young Hughie coming towards the house in the company of his brother James, aged 28, and his married sister Margaret Smith, aged 22. The family had heard that Hugh had been in a fight and they had been sent to bring him home, giving him hell as they did so.

Hugh's girlfriend, who had given birth to his child, was staying in the Murray house at the time and from a window she said she saw three members of the family walking down the garden path towards the front door with the detectives. She said that at the door, Hugh tried to get into the house but was prevented from entering by one of the officers.

DC Hair confirmed this, saying, 'I grabbed the waistband of his trousers and pulled him back from the top step. At that moment something struck me from behind. I do not know what it was. I kept hold of Hugh who started to struggle violently and I found myself being pinned back on a hedge with him on top of me. He tried to gouge at my left eye and was punching me.'

And so, apparently, began the battle of Earn Gardens. Like all battles, large and small, it was confusing and bloody. No one could be sure exactly what was happening during every moment of the violent mêlée. Lasting between five and ten minutes, it involved the four police officers on one side and Hugh Murray, his father (who had been at the door), his two brothers and his sister on the other. According to the police, the attack was completely unprovoked and they were unarmed. According to the Murrays, the police were heavy-handed, were using batons and had not identified themselves. Hugh Murray junior said he thought they were relatives of the boy he had stabbed earlier, come to exact revenge.

William Murray, 20, heard the ruckus outside his front door and flew down the stairs from his bedroom, wearing only a pair of underpants. Police say he joined the fray armed with two poles, looking, according to one of the officers, 'like a samurai warrior'.

DC Hair finally managed to get away from young Hugh to see DS Hunt locked in a struggle with the boy's father at the gate. He said he heard the sergeant shouting, 'Right, lads, back to the cars.' and there was a temporary lull as all four policemen began to retreat warily back to their vehicles. Blood was streaming down DC Hair's face from the wounds on his head and he could see Margaret Smith standing behind her father. Then, he said, the older man lunged at DS Hunt again and the fighting began once more.

'I made to Mr Murray [senior] and kicked him between the legs,' said the police officer, 'but the father got hold of Mr Hunt and they began struggling again.'

DC Wilson Gillan said he saw DS Hunt grappling with both Hugh Murray senior and junior as well as with Margaret Smith. He said the older man was trapped below the detective sergeant, who was in turn being held down by the younger Hugh Murray, straddling his body. Then, he said, he saw Margaret Smith move in with something long and thin in her hand and stab it into the policeman's legs. 'It went right in up to her hand,' he said. 'I don't know if it was a blade. I couldn't say.'

DC Gillan said he tried to get to DS Hunt but was forced back by one of the brothers who was battering him across the head with a pole. As he fought, he said he heard DS Hunt shout, 'I've been stabbed. They've got knives.' (In court, DC Gillan agreed under questioning by defence counsel that the incident had been the cause of great grief among fellow officers and had been much discussed before the trial. However, he said he doubted if these discussions would have coloured his evidence, but admitted 'there is always that possibility'.)

DC Hair also tried to help the older officer but was struck over the back of the head by a weapon. He recalled seeing Margaret Smith trying to pull her father away from DS Hunt. Then he ran to the police car to radio for assistance. When he had done so and moved back into the fray, he was confronted by William Murray 'lashing about with a clothes pole' and by James Murray who, armed with a broom handle, was fighting with the other detectives. Then he heard someone shout 'I've been stabbed!' but could not tell who it was.

'I saw young Hugh Murray leaving the shoulder of DS Hunt and he came towards me with a knife in his hand. It was a small knife. He ran towards me slashing the knife and shouting, "I'll kill you, you bastard!" and I ran back from him. Then Hugh veered from me and ran towards the house.'

The noise of the fight had alerted neighbours and a number of them were drawn to their windows and then to their phones to contact the police. One neighbour said she saw 50-year-old Hugh Murray beating a man on the ground with a stick. The man was rolling around and was face down as he tried to pull himself to safety but, according to the witness, was stopped by Mr Murray who was kicking him. She said she also heard Margaret Smith say, 'Give me the fucking thing. The bastard broke my glasses,' before taking the pole and beginning to hammer at the man on the ground and then to kick him so ferociously that the man's body rose from the ground with the force of the blow.

'I heard the man groaning and he appeared to be unconscious when Margaret had finished with him,' said the neighbour, adding that she had to look away because the scene was so horrific.

After Hugh junior had run away, DC Hair said he tried once again to get to DS Hunt but found Margaret Smith standing over the officer, also with a knife clutched in her hand, screaming at him, 'You've got my father. Leave my father alone, you bastard!' DC Hair looked and saw the older Hugh lying underneath DS Hunt. The man managed to crawl out from under the injured sergeant and ran towards the house, followed by his daughter. DS Hunt was moaning and when DC Hair moved to help him he found his skin cold and clammy.

DC Nicolson had also tried to help the downed officer. He had come upon Murray senior fighting with the sergeant as they lay on the ground and had stood on the man's hand to try and stop him punching his colleague. That was when William Murray came running down the path with two poles in his hands, 'looking like a samurai warrior', and handed one to his brother, James. DC Nicolson then described how he struggled with this brother, saying he felt the man's fingers go into his left eye as he said, 'I'm going to kill you, you polis bastard.' And then he, too, was stabbed.

'I could see a young boy creeping down the side of the house with something in his hand that glinted like stainless steel or chrome,' he said. 'I saw him go for my leg and then felt an intense heat and pain in my right leg and then the same thing happened to my shoulder.'

Hugh Murray junior admitted that he had stabbed DS Hunt, but insisted it was an accident. He said he had run out of the house with the knife, which he had taken from the kitchen, after he saw his father fighting with one of the men – who he insisted had not identified themselves as police officers. He said he could see another two men moving forward and he told the one fighting his father to get away from him. He was holding the knife out in front of him to frighten them off. 'I had the knife in front of me,' he said, 'but he breenged forward to grab me. He pulled me towards him . . .'

He said the knife just seemed to go into the man and he staggered back, then lunged forward again to grab him. 'The two of us fell down to the ground,' he said. 'I still had the knife in my hand and ran away.' He said the knife might also have gone into the officer as they fell. He also said that he ran at a man struggling with his brother, James, and began to punch him. He was still holding the knife but at the time did not know he had stabbed the man.

A neighbour told how she saw Mr Murray lying underneath a man on the ground and then saw young Hughie standing with a knife, the blade of which was pointed down. Then he ran into a garden and the witness said she heard a woman's voice shouting, 'Get rid of the knife! The polis are coming!'

Whatever happened that night, the simple fact was that DS Hunt lay dying from a number of stab wounds, DC Nicolson had been injured on the leg and shoulder and the other two officers had both been beaten with sticks. Police officers who arrived at the garden after the fight was over said that it looked like 'a scene from a war movie'. Bits of fencing and poles lay in the garden and blood was smeared on the ground. The shocked officers swiftly sealed off the cul-de-sac and began house-to-house inquiries as DS Hunt was rushed the ten miles to Law Hospital. The ambulance was given a police escort to speed its progress.

During the journey the injured man stopped breathing and an ambulanceman had to create an airway in his throat while his colleague radioed ahead to warn doctors of the change in the patient's condition. On arrival he was given external cardiac massage and mouth-to-mouth resuscitation until an anaesthetist arrived to give him oxygen. He had lost 75 per cent of his blood through six stab wounds and various incisions on his chest, body and thighs.

Three and half hours later, a surgeon who had arrived to operate discovered that the man had a tear in his liver and one blow had pierced a lung. DS Hunt died at 6.00 a.m. Doctors said that nothing could have saved him. He had been less than a year away from retiring, having served 30 years with the force.

DC Nicolson was also in a serious condition, with a collapsed lung. It took him some months to recover fully.

Police arrested Hugh Murray senior, his wife, Jean, Margaret Smith, James and William Murray at their home in Earn Gardens. William Murray was still dressed only in his underpants and a young police-constable handcuffed him and placed him in the rear of a police vehicle. In court, this officer confirmed that he could see no injuries on the young man's face and denied seeing a detective punch Murray on the nose. However, Murray's nose *was* fractured and the officer agreed that if that was the case it must have happened after he was placed in the police car.

Hugh Murray junior had sloped off into the night and a full-scale search was launched immediately. Shortly after 4 a.m. a detective sergeant caught sight of a youth running through the gardens of Robert Smillie Crescent, half a mile away from Earn Gardens. The detective climbed out of his car and chased him on foot. The young man, naked from the waist up, stopped and faced the pursuing officer, his hands raised above his head. 'All right, it's me you're after,' he said. 'Don't hurt me.' The police officer said that the young man stated his name was Hugh Murray, saying, 'I wish I could say it wasn't. How's my ma and da?'

Murray was told that his family had been arrested and he apparently replied, 'It was me. Don't blame them. I don't know what made me stab them. I just went crazy.'

Later, as he was taking them to the banks of the River Avon to find a 'tattie knife' which he said he had thrown into a gully, young Hugh was said to have asked, 'What do you think I'll get – four years, maybe?' Police claimed he also said, 'I must be crazy to stab polis.' The knife was never found.

Other family members also made statements to the police. Hugh Murray senior is alleged to have said, 'Look, I've never been in trouble in my life but when I saw the CID struggling with my family, I had to jump in.' He said he did not use a knife. 'I just grabbed one of them from the back, throwing my arms around him and we both fell to the ground. He just lay there and when I stood up I was hit with a baton.' He continued, 'I can't believe it. I didn't do it, so it must've been one of the others who was doing the stabbing.' Then he asked the officer interviewing him, 'I suppose you think I'm an animal?'

Margaret Smith was also making a statement, the police said, but she refused to sign it. 'The polis grabbed our Hughie,' the statement read. 'I ran into my ma's house. They were all at the door and everything just blew up. I saw one of them hit my father. I jumped on him. I wasn't having that so I had a go at the polis. I tried to get them off my father but they wouldn't come off.' Then she apparently said, perhaps in response to a question, 'Stab him? Who said I stabbed him? Anyway, you bastards prove I had a knife; prove who did the stabbing.'

James Murray was telling the police, 'I was walking to my mother's house with my brother, Hugh, and Margaret. Hugh had been in trouble fighting early on and I was taking him to my mother's house. When we got there we were stopped by four plainclothes polis who said they were looking for Hugh. I said, "Wait till I see my father," and we all went into the house.'

After that, James said he heard his father arguing with someone. 'That was when the fighting started. I was fighting with a big fellow with a moustache and got "cawed" over a garden hedge, and I was fighting with another guy. I don't know what I did then.' The next thing he remembered was sitting on his doorstep and asking someone for a cigarette.

William Murray apparently said in his interview, 'I ran downstairs. I did nothing, honest. The polis just came then and I got handcuffed and put in a polis motor. I wasn't out of the house for two seconds when I got put in the motor.'

All six members of the family were ultimately charged with the police officer's murder and assaults on the other three detectives. But that situation would quite rightly change. The trial began on Monday, 19 September 1983, in the High Court of Glasgow and within four days Jean Murray was cleared of DS Hunt's murder and other charges of assaulting the police. Mrs Murray was a highly respected person in the town, being described as a kind, caring person. She was a registered home help with the local district council with an enviable reputation for helping others above and beyond the call of duty.

By the end of the trial, Margaret Smith would also be acquitted of attempting to murder DC Nicolson but still faced the charge of murdering DS Hunt along with her father and three brothers. Both she and young Hugh were pleading self-defence.

Hugh Murray senior said in court that his wife wakened him, explaining that there were men at the door looking for young Hugh. He said his wife told him she did not know who they were. When he went to the door, he saw his son, James, running down the footpath with two men behind him. 'There was another man at the gate with his back to me,' he told the court. 'I put my hand on his shoulder and said "What's going on?" There was a struggle and I was pushed to the ground. I remember being kicked in the face and hip.'

His defence counsel asked him if any of the men identified themselves as police by showing him a warrant card or even saying they were CID. Hugh Murray said they did not, and denied hitting anyone with a weapon.

'If you had seen your 16-year-old boy with a knife, what would you have done?' he was asked.

'My God, sir, I don't know,' said Mr Murray, adding, 'I didn't allow quarrelling or fighting. I tried to bring my family up the best way I could.'

Margaret Smith, on the other hand, admitted that she hit DS Hunt once or twice with a stick. She was, she said, trying to help her father break free from the man. She echoed her brother's testimony when she said she'd thought the four men who approached them outside their home that night were people looking for young Hugh because of the fight. She said one of the men grabbed her young brother and when she went to help him was warned, 'If he gets away, you will get what he is going to get.'

She said she was scared and, as she was trying to get into the house, her father appeared and asked what was going on. Then the fighting started. Her father was knocked to the ground, she said, and while he was being kicked someone hit her across the side of the head. The blow broke her glasses. She said that she never had a knife in her hand at any time during the struggle.

James Murray confirmed that his brother, Hugh, appeared with a knife just as he was knocked over a wall. He told the court that he shouted 'Get on down the road!' to his brother. He did not see Hugh do anything with the knife but did say that the man which whom he was fighting suddenly stopped punching him and released him. James was eventually cleared of killing DS Hunt, but still faced a charge of assaulting the dead man.

The trial lasted 15 days. The court heard that blood which was found on a bent kitchen knife and on the handle of a longer knife could have come from the dead officer; and stains on a t-shirt and a woman's grey cardigan, which were found at the scene, were also traced to DS Hunt. Whereas blood discovered on three pieces of fencing post could have come from DC Nicolson.

The prosecution reminded the jury that Hugh Murray junior had picked up two knives in the kitchen and ran out, with one witness saying that he pointed one at DS Hunt. His father had been seen kicking and hitting the policeman with a piece of stick. One of the detectives present had seen Margaret Smith not only striking DS Hunt with a pole but also making some sort of stabbing motion at his leg. However, Margaret Smith's counsel argued that the detectives' evidence was contradictory – one had said that he saw something shining in her hand, while the other said she had something dark and dull. He also said that one of the detectives spoke of Mrs Smith making a 'prodding' motion, although the pathologist said it would take at least three knife blows to cause the injuries on the dead man's legs.

The jury were also assured that the detectives had identified themselves as police officers by showing a warrant card. The defence insisted that the officers had *not* identified themselves. Hugh Murray junior claimed that he stabbed DS Hunt accidentally.

William Murray was the third member of the family to have the murder charge against him dropped. The announcement was made to the jury in the latter stages of the trial, prompting his counsel to observe that he was 'astonished' that it took so long for his client to be cleared as there was clearly no evidence that he had even assaulted the officer.

Finally, despite the gallant efforts of their counsel, the jury took three and a half hours to find Hugh Murray junior unanimously Guilty and his father and sister Guilty by a majority of murdering DS Hunt. The father and daughter were sentenced to life, while the young son, being under 18, was detained without limit of time. He also received seven years for the attempted murder of DC Nicolson. James was given three years for assaulting DC Nicolson. William Murray was cleared of all charges.

The question which hangs over the entire senseless affair is what made a normally quiet and law-abiding family go berserk and attack four police officers. Young Hugh was a known trouble-maker at school and under-age drinker. But his father, brothers and sister, Margaret, had not been in trouble before. There was no history of alcohol problems in the Murray household, with Mr Murray spending much of his spare time training and racing grey-hounds. What made them do what they did? Struggling with officers is one thing, but to apparently pick up sticks and beat them is another. So what happened that night?

On passing sentence, the trial judge, Lord Robertson, com-mented on how Hugh Murray junior had ruined the lives of a number of people. This was true. He had wrecked not only his own family but also that of Ross Hunt, whose wife told the press she had wanted her husband's killers to hang. The dead man's son, Adrian, was a cadet with Strathclyde Police and said he would continue in his chosen career, to make his father proud of him.

In Hamilton Police Station, there is a plaque honouring DS Hunt. Directly beside it is another plaque dedicated to another Lanarkshire officer, PC George Taylor, who was murdered by Robert Mone and Thomas McCulloch as they broke out of the State Hospital at Carstairs in 1976. But more of that later . . .

Forbidden Love

BILL AND BOB

THE ATTITUDES of certain tabloid newspapers apart, homosexuals are now more accepted in modern western society. The laws relating to them are more liberal than they have ever been, although the legal age of consent is 18, two years above that set for heterosexuals. (This is currently the subject of an appeal in Europe, claiming the ruling discriminates between sexes.)

But it was not always so. In Oscar Wilde's day, homosexuals had to indulge their sexual preferences behind the veil of apparent 'respectability', often using a marriage and children as a shield. The authorities knew it was going on – in fact, many major establishment figures were probably personally involved – but tended to ignore it unless a public figure was somewhat indiscreet (in Wilde's case becoming caught up in an embarrassing and highly public liaison with a nobleman's son). Then hypocrisy – a way of life, if not invented by the Victorians, then certainly refined by them – came to the fore and the establishment would band together to condemn the love that dare not speak its name. Meanwhile, some of those self-same establishment figures continued to enjoy themselves behind their own veneer of respectability with prostitutes, little girls, little boys or farmyard animals. Nowadays, of course, politicians preach of making a return to traditional Victorian values, as if the morality of that age is something to admire.

But this attitude was not solely the province of Great Britain. In Russia, during the same period, Tchaikovsky found it difficult to come to terms with his own homosexuality and finally may have taken his own life because of it. The composer lived his life terrified that his sexual orientation would reach his public and so destroy his reputation. If word got out, his work would never be performed in polite society, and in those days that meant his work would never be played.

His homosexual leanings, like many of his contemporaries, began to manifest themselves while at school, in his case the St Petersburg School of Jurisprudence, where many students had their first experience of sex with fellow students. In fact, the school was well known in its day for its extra-curricular homosexual activities.

From then on, although he tried to follow convention and strike up relationships with women, Tchaikovsky's anxiety over his sexuality increased. In 1893 – after he received an honorary degree from Cambridge, an honour which he would not have been accorded had his private life been made public – Tchaikovsky died of cholera five days after the first public performance of his Sixth Symphony, the 'Pathetique', which is said to reflect his feelings of guilt and anxiety.

It is said that he committed suicide by drinking contaminated water, unable to cope with his double life any longer. Then there is another theory: that he was forced to drink it by some of his old schoolfriends who had now become part of society, having apparently cast off their old practices, and were outraged that one of their own had continued in them. But that could merely be a rumour, like Mozart being murdered by the jealous Salieri. Whatever the truth, Tchaikovsky's brother, Modest, also homosexual, destroyed many of the composer's private letters and papers, so the world will never know just how sexually active the man was.

This feeling of suspicion and abhorrence continued into the twentieth century, perhaps reaching a peak in Nazi Germany, when homosexuals were herded up along with other 'sub-standard' species, like Jews and gypsies, and put into concentration camps, where some fine, upstanding Aryans indulged in discreet and decidedly non-Aryan sexual athletics before sending them to the gas chamber. The latter final solution perhaps being something those who screech stridently about the Gay Plague would like to do today.

Gays may be more readily accepted in these more liberal times but old attitudes, like old soldiers, never die but merely fade away. For all our liberality, the public at large still carry deep suspicions and prejudices. In the forties and fifties, husky male film stars hid their predilections from their public. Politicians still do. And if you are a headmaster and the parents of your charges – or a local newspaper – catch a whiff of any impropriety, then God help you! For, liberal laws apart, if you are 'queer' then you must be a pervert and the young boys are therefore at risk. It is not true, of course, and there is just as much chance – perhaps even more – of a heterosexual teacher turning lascivious eyes on the young girls in his class.

Criminal annals are riddled with cases of homosexuals being attacked by 'straights'. Even in this so-called enlightened age, 'queer bashing' can still go on outside some public toilets and those pubs which cater solely for gay customers. Occasionally, these attacks can turn into murder. And because many gays still lead secret double lives – married with families but sneaking out to fulfil their sexual desires with other men – they can be open to blackmail. In 1993, a Glasgow man was jailed for three years for blackmailing homosexuals in the city, while the Glasgow City Liaison Group was set up specifically to advise and assist gays throughout the country who are open to blackmail. In the first 18 months of their existence, they received over 6,000 calls for help.

Similarly, within eight hours of one particular killing in Glasgow in November 1993, the organisation received 260 calls from worried gays who felt that there was a killer stalking the city streets targeting homosexuals. The victim in that particular case was one of the city's procurator fiscals – the official prosecutors – and his death, as well as the manner of it, raised headlines for weeks.

Marshall Stormonth was a discreet homosexual who has been described by colleagues as an excellent lawyer. News of his violent death hit the Glasgow legal profession – on both the prosecution and defence sides – like a thunderbolt. On the night of 17 November 1993 he went out with friends and colleagues for a meal and a drink at the Tron Theatre, leaving at just after 11 p.m., ostensibly to go home and do some work. However, he did not go straight home. Instead, he was seen at between 11 and 11.30 p.m. at a carpark near Kelvingrove Park, one of Glasgow's better-known pick-up points for gays. Over the years, there have been a number of reports of gay bashing in the area of University Avenue, the tree-lined road which runs through the park to Argyle Street.

Just after midnight, a resident who lived next to Mr Stormonth's flat at 3 Botanic Crescent in the west end reported hearing noises and stamping from the flat. Then there was the unmistakable crackle of flames and smoke belched from doors and windows. When firemen broke into the flat they found the procurator fiscal dead, his hands and feet bound together. It was subsequently discovered that he had been battered with a champagne bottle and then been throttled, first with a tie and then a belt. Then his killer – or killers as it turned out – set fire to the flat to destroy any evidence. Palm and fingerprints, however, were found in the hallway outside and further prints on an armchair in the flat.

Investigations soon led police to two brothers, Steven and Dean Ryan, aged 21 and 17 respectively. Steven had been boasting about the murder to a girl and her boyfriend, even demonstrating how he had tightened the tie around the man's neck, saying he watched his face turn purple. He said that he and his brother had met Mr Stormonth in a bar and had pretended to be gay so that they could lure him back to his flat and rob him. The idea was to take his bank cash-card, which they did but could not get any cash. They also took a set of keys and four pounds in cash. Dean first hit him with the bottle, then Steven began to choke him with the tie, wrapping it round his neck as he lay face down on the carpet and pulling it tight as he pressed down with his foot on the man's back. But the tie broke and he repeated the process with a belt, finally killing him. Then they set fire to the flat to destroy any clues. Steven Ryan had also confessed to his grandmother and an aunt.

In March 1994, the two brothers were sentenced to life in prison for the brutal murder.

But homosexuals are not only killed by 'straights', they can also kill each other. They are, after all, just like everyone else and, like everyone else, can find the time to kill. Murder is an equal-opportunity crime.

And then there are those cases where it is difficult to tell exactly what happened, because the records of the day drip with disapproval over the victim's lifestyle.

In years gone by, the cobblestones of Park Terrace Lane in Glasgow's fashionable west end echoed to the sound of horses' hooves and the rumble of carriage wheels. But by the 1950s the former stables at number 43 had been converted into a garage and the coachman's apartments above into a flat. It was here that William Vincent lived a tastefully decorated life while running his successful business below. But the dapper, bespectacled little man had a secret, known only to a select few. He was a homosexual with a taste for young men. Had his tastes ran to young women he might have been called, with some affection or even envy, a bit of a lad. As it was, he became known after his death as a corrupter of young flesh and a danger to public morals, and nobody – apart from a few friends and family – seemed to mourn his passing.

Early in 1954 he met 17-year-old Robert Scott at the Graham Square car market in Glasgow's east end. Vincent spotted the handsome youngster as he sat at a coffee bar and sat down in front of him, striking up a conversation. They talked pleasantly enough and the young man left him there. It would be four months before they met again and begin a friendship that would leave the young man wracked with guilt and self-disgust.

In the period between, Robert moved to London in search of his fortune. The lure of the great city to the south, where the streets are still believed to be effectively paved with gold, has proved too strong for many a Scottish youngster. Robert soon found out that the metropolis did not hold the promise of riches he first thought, and returned to Glasgow, where he met up again with William Vincent.

It was now the summer of 1954 and Robert Scott was alone at a St Vincent Street coffee stall, in the city centre, when William Vincent saw him again and recognised him as the youngster he had first noticed, and no doubt taken a fancy to, at the car market all those weeks before. He began chatting to him again. Or chatting him up. Young Robert may have known what was going on or he may not, there is now no way of telling. But whatever the case, the older man asked him if he wanted to have another coffee.

Scott shook his head and glanced at his watch. 'No thanks,' he said. 'I've got to run and catch my bus home . . .'

Vincent smiled and replied, 'There's no rush. I've got the car and I'll run you home. There's plenty of time.'

But Robert wanted to get home and he made his apologies. Vincent suggested that they meet the following day, a Saturday, and go out for a drink. Robert agreed and they arranged to meet in a city-centre pub. By keeping that appointment, Robert Scott and William Vincent took the first steps towards murder.

The two men had some drinks in the city centre before moving up west to the Crocodile Club in Park Circus, not far from Vincent's mews flat in Park Terrace Lane. All the time, the young man was drinking steadily and growing gradually more and more drunk. Eventually, Vincent told him there was no need for him to go all the way home to the east end. He could come and stay the night at his place. After all, it was only round the corner . . .

Robert Scott stayed the night, sleeping in Vincent's bed. He later said that he was so drunk he could not remember what – if anything – happened that night.

But whatever happened, Vincent became increasingly infatuated with the young man, while Robert seemed to return the friendship – even taking the older man to meet his parents in their Forge Street home, near Parkhead. He introduced his new friend as Bill and the man set out to impress Mr and Mrs Scott, taking them for runs in his gleaming Jaguar, inviting them to tea in his posh west-end flat, flashing his money at every possible opportunity. He said he wanted to set young Bob up in business, maybe even make him a partner in his own company. He talked big and he spent big, and tried to buy his way into their confidence.

Despite being thrilled at the opportunities being proferred to their boy, William Scott sensed something was wrong with Bill. He did not trust him completely and felt he was bad for his son. Robert was spending too much time with the man, for instance, and there seemed to be something too good to be true about the businessman. Something, perhaps, a little unsavoury.

As time wore on, Robert himself began to grow disenchanted with Bill. He angrily left the room on one occasion when Bill and some like-minded friends were passing around obscene photographs of naked young men. And one night, Bill made a pass at the young man as he slept in his bed in Park Terrace Lane. Robert coldly told him, 'Don't think I am like those other pals that you know.' William Vincent apologised and said nothing like that would ever happen again. Finally, the icing was definitely wearing off the gingerbread as Robert turned bitterly to his parents and said, 'Don't let him know you are poor. He'll hate you for it.'

The boy's father began to notice a change in his son's demeanour. He was normally a fairly happy young man with a smile for everyone, but gradually, as what William Scott saw as an unhealthy friendship developed, Robert's moods changed, veering dramatically from happy to unstable. It could be that the young man was battling with his own natural urges, and William Vincent, an older and more experienced man, may have recognised this in him. And as things progressed perhaps Scott could not accept what he really was. This was 1950s Britain after all, and these things were not accepted. Society was conditioned to believe that homosexuality was an affront to nature and Robert – like many another young man before and since – may have been finding it difficult to balance these teachings with his own inclinations. That might explain why he remained Vincent's friend even though he knew the man was homosexual, sharing his bed on more than one occasion, when convention would have demanded that he have nothing to do with him.

Or it could have merely been that Robert Scott had said to hell with convention. Perhaps at this time he genuinely liked Vincent as a purely platonic friend, and that friendship became almost an obsession with Vincent. Scott said he thought that the man could change – a common, misguided belief among heterosexuals, that homosexuals are just wrong-headed individuals who merely need the love of someone of the opposite sex to bring them to their senses. And then there was that offer of a partnership to think about. Scott was a young man, with ambitions and the future to consider.

In 1955, Scott was called up for National Service and was eventually posted to 16 Company, RAOC, based at Longtown in Cumberland. During his time in the service, Vincent continued to write to him, crossing kisses at the bottom of each letter, telling him how much he missed him and saying how he longed to be with him.

In June 1957, Vincent visited Scott in Cumberland and the young soldier met him in the hotel in which he was going to stay the night. Vincent asked Bob to come up to his room to wait for him while he changed. Scott agreed and followed him up the stairs, but when they arrived in the room Vincent suddenly turned and kissed him. Scott felt 'terrible and disgusted'.

Scott began to distance himself from Vincent. He stopped replying to his letters, eventually prompting Vincent to write to his commanding officer asking why the young man did not write back. He also wrote to the colonel requesting information about buying Robert out of the Army. Vincent was distraught. He wanted his friend back by his side.

However, Vincent was not a monk. Bob might be away but he still had his needs and in 1957 he picked up a youth in a Glasgow pub, took him home and afterwards gave him a job. The young man, who had recently moved to the city from Dundee, worked for Vincent for a fortnight before he turned on him, battering him with a piece of rubber tubing, binding his wrists and then tying them to his legs, gagging him with a handkerchief and a cravat before making off with a ring, a watch and £116.10s in cash, which was a great deal of money in those days. The attack generated another letter from Vincent to Scott's commander, this time asking him if the young man could get leave in order to come home and help him get over his ordeal. Scott did not go home to help.

Scott was finally discharged from the Army in January 1958. Somehow, Vincent got wind of his return and was at the railway station to meet him. He was delighted to see his friend, but his delight turned to anger when Scott told him that he wanted to go home and see his parents.

'He seemed to want me all to himself,' said Scott.

Once back in Glasgow, it was not so easy to disentangle himself from Vincent's influence. But he was determined he wanted no more to do with him. He told Vincent to his face that he wanted to strike out on his own, that he did not wish to be a part of the man's life or his lifestyle. He handed back the gold cigarette case, inscribed 'to Bob Scott', which Vincent had once presented to him. He told him not to write to him, ever again. Not to phone him. Not to talk to him.

But it did not work.

The letters and the phone calls and the pleas to see him kept coming. Vincent even threatened to tell his parents all about their son – and what he got up to in Vincent's bed. Finally, in March 1958, Robert and his parents went to see Vincent in his flat. Scott told him again that he did not wish to see him. Vincent refused to accept it and an argument erupted. Things were said in the heat of anger and Robert finally stormed from the flat, saying he did not wish to see any of them again. He went to stay with a friend. Scott's parents were never to see him as a free man again. Vincent would see him once more. To his cost.

Scott had said he wanted to make his own way and he was doing just that. He found a job as a salesman and was doing very well. He also worked in the evenings as a waiter in a bar on New City Road. But Vincent would not stop pestering him and one night, Saturday, 12 April 1958 – five weeks after the row in the flat – Scott finished work at about quarter to eleven and went to a late-night club for a coffee. It was a place often frequented by Vincent and the young man hoped he would see him there so that he could tell him one last time to leave him alone, to stop writing letters which he never read and making phone calls he did not take. But Vincent was not there that night and Scott, determined to see this thing through, phoned him at his flat. Vincent told him that if he wanted to speak to him he should come up and see him. Scott agreed to go. He did not know it then, but he was making a grave mistake.

He made his way to the flat in the Victorian lane, the half-light cast by the flickering gaslamps sending his shadow shivering on the bare brick walls around him, and knocked on the door. Vincent let him in, closing the door behind him. Scott began to say something but Vincent did what he always did – he threw his arms around the young man and held him close, trying to kiss him. But this time it went wrong. This time Scott did not just push himself away in disgust. This time something snapped inside Scott's mind. This time he reacted angrily and violently. He pushed Vincent away and reached up with his left hand, wrapping his fingers around his throat and began to squeeze. Vincent struggled in the grip, trying to break free but Scott had really had enough now; now it was over and he was going to show him.

He did not mean to kill William Vincent, merely to show him just how revolted and angry he was at the whole affair. But kill him he did, choking the life out of him, his fingernails digging deeply into the man's flesh and drawing blood. Vincent stopped struggling and hung limply in his former young friend's hands before slumping to the floor. Shocked, Scott dropped to the man's side and felt for a pulse but found no beat. William Vincent was dead. And he had killed him.

Blood was oozing from the four wounds on the neck and without thinking, Scott looked around for something to put on them. For some reason, which made sense only to Scott's panicked mind, he took one of Vincent's socks off and placed it round the neck to staunch the blood flow. And then it really began to sink in. He had killed someone. It was murder. He had not meant to do it but he had. And he would have to cover it up somehow.

Vincent's car, a 1956 yellow and red Sunbeam Talbot Alpine, was in the garage below. Scott dragged the body downstairs and into the garage, hauling it across the dusty floor by the legs. Then he opened the car boot and bundled the corpse inside before climbing into the driving seat and roaring out of the mews garage, the wheels bouncing over the cobbles which covered the narrow lane. He did not know where he was going, all he knew was that he had to get away from the city – somewhere, anywhere – and dump the body.

Finally he drove 90 miles to the place he had first felt safe from Vincent's influence – Longtown in Cumberland, where he had been stationed. He drove all night, finally reaching Blackbank Wood where he intended to dispose of the body. Afterwards he could drive away again, leaving Vincent and the whole sordid affair behind him. Then, perhaps, he could start his life afresh. But it was not to be.

Scott made the mistake of turning the car off the small road and actually going into the forest. Perhaps he did not want to risk anyone noticing the car parked at the roadside – a yellow and red sports car is not the most unobtrusive of vehicles. Whatever his reason, he soon found himself bogged down in a muddy ditch about 20 yards from the road.

It is possible Scott realised then his dreams of a new life free from Vincent's attentions were to be dashed. Or maybe he thought he could continue to bluff it out, for he walked the short distance to the Army base guardhouse and asked the corporal on duty if he could get help in pulling his car out of the ditch. The corporal said there was no help available just at that moment. Scott thought about his predicament for a time before finally reaching a decision and asked if he could use the telephone. The corporal pointed it out to him and left him to make what was undoubtedly the most fateful phone call of his life.

Scott asked to be connected to the police office in Gretna and told the surprised officer who answered, 'I have done a murder. If you come to the 16th Company guardroom, I will show you a body.'

The report was passed on to Longtown Police and Sergeant Edward Waiting left there at 5.25 a.m. to investigate. But things were not moving quickly enough for Scott, who by now wanted the whole thing over and done with, and he phoned Gretna again, asking where the police officers were. He was told an officer was on his way and to wait there. Shortly after that second call, Sergeant Waiting walked into the guardroom and asked Scott if he was the gentleman who had phoned Gretna about a murder. Scott nodded and told the sergeant to take him to the wood. They climbed into the police car and went back to the spot, just off the Longtown to Gretna road, where the car lay stuck in the mud, a blaze of colour in the dark greens and browns of the surrounding fir-trees. Scott pointed to the boot and the policeman sprung the lock.

The body lay curled up inside, the knees up to the chest, facing the interior of the car, wearing a shirt, trousers and only one sock. The other bloodstained sock was still wrapped round the neck. There was also a dark mark on the shoulders, left there when Scott dragged the corpse across the dirty garage floor to the car boot. When searched further, Vincent's body was found to have £232 in used notes in his pocket.

The sergeant alerted CID and Scott was taken away to Longtown Police Station, while officers sealed off the area around the car and began taking their measurements and photographs. On the way, Scott sadly told his escort, 'I have saved some people a lot of misery.'

In Longtown, while detectives went through Scott's belongings, he told them to keep a handkerchief to one side, apparently saying that he tried to strangle Vincent with it, 'but it had not been strong enough so I used a sock instead'. Later, in court, he would deny this, saying that he throttled the man with his hands and used the sock to mop up the blood from the wounds.

While Scott sat dejectedly in the police station, Glasgow CID was contacted and informed of the grim discovery. Police immediately rushed to Vincent's flat and found traces of blood on the floor just behind the door and also the wide drag mark in the dirt in the garage. In the wardrobe, they found the jacket belonging to the suit trousers on the corpse. Neighbours told of hearing the noise of a struggle and the car leaving the lane early on Sunday morning. A friend of Vincent's arrived, looking for the man but finding a uniformed constable on the door. He explained he had arranged to meet the dead man and when he had not shown up had come around to find out what was wrong. And gradually, they unearthed the sometimes sordid life of the man neighbours regarded as a kindly bachelor known to show consideration to local children when they were ill – although one neighbour had noted that he never seemed to have any women friends, only male.

While investigators dug into Vincent's background in Glasgow, detectives travelled to Longtown to pick up the suspect. He was driven back overnight to Scotland in a police car, his head encompassed in a blanket whenever in the public gaze, while another officer followed in the Sunbeam. The small convoy arrived at Partick Police Station – then known as the Marine because it had responsibility for part of the north bank of the Clyde – at about 10 a.m. on Monday morning, and Scott was charged with murder at 1.18 p.m. He told officers, 'He tried to ruin my life and make me the same as him.'

At first, his parents had heard only that there had been a murder in the west end and that the body had been found in a car boot. Then they heard the name of the victim – and that their son had been arrested in England trying to dispose of the body. On the night of the murder, they had been across the city enjoying a quiet little anniversary dinner, totally unaware that Robert was committing murder in the west end. The day after his arrival in Glasgow, Mr Scott visited Robert in his cell, but the young man did not wish to talk to him. At a loss over what to say, the stunned father asked his son if he had enough cigarettes. The young man turned away and said, 'Yes, plenty, just leave me alone.'

His trial, which was held in April, lasted only two days. Details of Vincent's life were examined, as was Scott's relationship with the man. The accused said that Vincent was both intelligent and very foolish, frequenting coffee stalls and late-night clubs, throwing his money about and giving it to people he did not know.

In the opinion of the trial judge, Lord Russell, William Vincent's death may merely have been the killing of a 'worthless' man, but reminded the jury of ten men and five women that 'this is not a court of morals but a court of law', meaning they had to put 'personal revulsion' aside in deciding over Scott's guilt or innocence. It did not matter how 'worthless' an individual the evidence might show William Vincent to be, no one had the right to set himself up as an executioner.

The jury was out for only 32 minutes before they returned a majority verdict of Guilty and Scott turned to face the bench for sentencing. He had been found guilty of murder and so could have faced the gallows. But the court had some sympathy with his situation and he was sentenced to life, although no minimum period was recommended. And so, Robert Scott was sent to Perth Prison to begin his sentence. Technically, he could have been let out again at any time, depending on the views or whims of the Secretary of State for Scotland. But he never left the prison alive.

What happened in the months leading up to November 1959 was never discovered. He had been doing well in prison, it seems. He was even happy, with a ready smile and a willingness to work. He was even hopeful of being released soon because his sentence was being reviewed due to the background to the case. His letters home displayed no trace of unhappiness. But there was something wrong. Something must have been getting him down, although no one knew what. Whatever it was, it forced him to take drastic action.

Everything seemed normal when, on the morning of Thursday, 5 November 1959, civilian plumber William Young locked Robert Scott into the prison workshop while he went to have his tea. This was normal practice and Scott, who had been working for him for almost one year, usually continued with his work until he returned. And Scott did just that, completing the task he was doing before tidying up. But then he climbed up on to a metal table, threw one end of a rope over a roof beam and secured the other end firmly. Finally, he placed the noose around his neck and jumped off.

William Young found him hanging there, dead, when he returned. He had only been away for eight minutes.

Perhaps Scott could live no longer with what he had done to William Vincent. Perhaps other prisoners, either knowing or believing he was homosexual, had made his life a misery in the halls. Or perhaps he was not as confident as he seemed of his sentence being cut and could not face an indeterminate period ahead in prison, staring at that little tent of blue which prisoners call sky. Whatever it was that forced the young man to take his own life, his father was in no doubt as to who was really to blame. As far as he was concerned, William Vincent's influence had reached from beyond the grave and murdered his son. 'That loathsome creature and the other corrupters who surrounded him,' he told reporters, 'they are the men responsible for his death.'

Robert Scott had found the High Court extremely sympathetic to his predicament, as did another man charged with the murder of a homosexual over 30 years later.

Friends of barman David Nicholls began to grow worried when they realised they had not heard from him for some time. He had left a dinner party early on 8 May 1990, saying he was tired and had not been seen since. On 11 May, two of his friends decided to visit Nicholls's flat at 4 Marywood Square in Strathbungo, on the south side of the city. They received no answer to their knock and thought about calling the police. The thing was, they had no reason to suspect anything was wrong, apart from the fact that they had not seen David for days. So, rather than raise the alarm needlessly, they forced their way into the house. They still ended up calling the police though.

David Nicholls lay on the living-room floor. He wore a white towelling robe, which gaped open at the front. He was naked underneath. Blood circled in a pool around his head and had dried on wounds on his face. One of his friends gently covered the body with the robe while the police and an ambulance were called.

A pathologist later found that the murdered 39-year-old man's skull was fractured on both sides, with a total of 27 wounds on the face and head. These wounds could have been caused by a hammer. In addition, three stab wounds to the neck had severed a main artery and the jugular. Death, the doctor announced, was caused by the stab wounds, although the blows to the head had also contributed.

Nicholls had made no secret of the fact that he was homo-sexual. He regularly frequented the city's gay bars and attended gay disco nights. During one of these he met a 26-year-old Dundee man. They liked each other and he took the man home with him. In April, he drove to Dundee in his silver B-registered BMW and helped his new lover move into his Glasgow flat.

But things did not go well. The lover had hoped that he and Nicholls would be able to forge a serious, long-term relationship. But within days of moving into the Strathbungo flat, he found that Nicholls had a tendency to tell lies and had something of a temper. The hoped-for serious relationship fizzled out and on Monday, 7 May, the man moved out again. At 4.00 p.m. that same day Nicholls left the flat to go to work in Caskies Bar in St Vincent Street. Later that night, his lover left the house keys at the bar, saying he would not be back. The following day, Nicholls went to the dinner party in Partick, in the west end. Some time between then and 11 May, he was murdered.

Detectives knew he had left the house in the west end at about 10.00 p.m. Half an hour later, he was then seen in the gay street market in St Vincent Street by rent boys, and then again driving his silver BMW towards the Kingston Bridge on-ramp. Police appealed to anyone who may have spoken to Nicholls after that time to come forward. The problem was, though, much of the gay community were proving reticent about coming forward. Many had kept their sex lives a secret from friends and family, and were fearful of any publicity involvement in a murder inquiry might bring. It is a problem common to both investigations of crimes involving gays and customers of prostitutes.

However, they did manage to gather enough information about Nicholls's life – including the fact that he would pay a rent boy £50 for a night of sex. They also interviewed 21-year-old former jockey Alan Duncan, who at first denied knowing the deceased – even though his fingerprints were found in his flat. But later, during the taped interview, Duncan broke down and confessed that he had killed the barman. There was, however, no suggestion of Alan Duncan being a homosexual.

Alan Duncan had called on Nicholls to talk to him about a job. But, perhaps like William Vincent over 30 years before, Nicholls had other ideas. Alan Duncan said that while he was in the

Strathbungo flat, Nicholls entered the room with his robe wide open, put his arms around him and kissed him, making his desire for sex quite plain. Duncan reared back and slapped Nicholls – then saw that he had a knife in his hand. Nicholls came at him, he said, and he tried to get away, picking up a hammer to keep him at bay. But he could not get away and, as Nicholls continued to advance on him with the knife, he struck out with the hammer.

Duncan repeated all this in court during his trial, breaking down in tears as he described the scene, weeping as he said that the two of them had struggled and in a panic he had grabbed the knife and stabbed Nicholls. When Nicholls released his hold and collapsed, Duncan fled from the flat, throwing the hammer and the knife away from a railway bridge on to the side of the tracks below. He later took police to the point where he had disposed of the weapons.

At his trial, Duncan claimed he had killed Nicholls in self-defence and eventually the Crown accepted this, reducing the original charge of murder to that of culpable homicide. The judge, Lord Kirkwood, said that the accused had acted under severe provocation and sentenced him to only six months in prison. The sentence was even more lenient than it sounds, for the judge back-dated it to when Duncan was first arrested, 26 June, which meant he would be a free man the week following the November trial.

There was no such leniency shown in the High Court of Edinburgh the following year, when a youth was sentenced to life for murdering an ex-army officer.

The naked body of Alex Colquhoun, a 51-year-old former Royal Artillery warrant officer and a caretaker with BBC Scotland in Edinburgh, was found stabbed to death in the bathroom of his home in Leith on Saturday, 28 December 1991. Again, the discovery was made by a worried friend who had not seen the man in days. When he entered the flat he found blood smeared on the walls and the carpet. The body had five major wounds – a large cut to his back and four on the front, including the fatal blow to the heart. Whatever happened, it was obvious the old soldier had gamely tried to fight off his attacker. As he had last been seen at a festive party in the city's Blue Oyster Club on Christmas Eve and had failed to meet friends on Christmas night as arranged, it was assumed the man had been lying there since Christmas morning.

The full-scale murder hunt adopted the tried and true methods of investigation – a mobile incident-room was set up outside Colquhoun's first-floor flat in Sandport Street, door-to-door inquiries were made and the area was saturated with officers looking for the murder weapon, checking buildings, gardens, roofs, drains, bins, play areas and waste ground in the immediate area. Building sites were also searched and bags of rubble – including those left by builders working in the victim's own tenement block – were tipped out and scrutinised.

Again, they appealed for help from the gay community and within days their investigations led them to two young men who had met Mr Colquhoun at the disco on Christmas Eve and went back with him to Leith in a taxi. Both men were charged with the murder but only one was found guilty, the charges against his friend being dropped.

Cameron Downie, aged 18, said that the older man had bought them drinks at the disco and later invited them to a party in his flat. What they did not know, it seems, was that there would only be themselves and him at the party. When they arrived at the Sandport Street flat, Mr Colquhoun made them something to eat and then put on a video featuring a triangle of men involved in gay sex. Downie said he grew bored with the video and fell asleep, leaving his friend and Mr Colquhoun sitting on the settee.

Some time later he was awakened by his friend calling out for help from the bedroom. He snatched a knife up from the kitchen and ran into the bedroom, finding, he said, Mr Colquhoun naked and pushing his friend down on to the bed. According to Downie, he was concerned for his pal's well-being and he ran to the bed, stabbing the older man in the back. The ex-soldier got up and started to come towards him, his hands reaching for Downie's throat. In terror for his own life, Downie said he stabbed the man again. And again. Until he was dead.

But Downie did not receive any of the leniency afforded to Alan Duncan in 1990 or Robert Scott in 1958. Lord Cameron of Lochbroom sentenced him to life, ordering that he be detained in a young offenders' institution.

Similarly, there was no such consideration for a man who killed another Edinburgh homosexual who, he claimed, had been trying to indecently assault him while he was asleep. He then hit the man 35 times over the head with a hammer, sword and an ornamental axe.

When police forced their way into the Tranent flat of 35-year-old James Arthur in October 1992, they found the battered and bloody body lying face down in the bedroom, wearing only a pair of boxer shorts, his left hand stretching out to a Bible lying a few feet away. They also found human tissue on a windowsill and a steel-shafted claw hammer beneath an outside stairway. There was blood on the hammer head.

John Martindale, a 25-year-old barman at a bingo hall, was subsequently arrested for the crime and, during his trial in February 1992, the court heard how he had met the deceased at Chapps late-night bar and then gone back to the flat in Church Street, Tranent. Martindale fell asleep but woke up to find the other man committing an 'indecent act' against him. The discovery sparked a flashback to when he was eight years old and being indecently assaulted by a man. His defence counsel said the memory acted 'like a time bomb' and he exploded, going berserk with rage, hitting and punching Arthur and finally beating him to death. Afterwards, inexplicably, Martindale sat in the flat and ate two bridies – a form of savoury meat pie – and even offered the corpse a cup of tea. This, coupled with the brutality of the murder, prompted one psychiatrist to describe Martindale's mental state as 'bordering on insanity'. The defence had been hoping – and had even asked – for a reduction of the murder charge to culpable homicide. It was not to be, though, and Martindale – who had previous convictions for violence – was found guilty and sentenced to life in prison.

England, too, has had its share of homosexual murderers and victims. Colin Ireland, for instance, was a London-based killer of homosexuals, although not homosexual himself. He did, however, have a penchant for sado-masochistic sex with girlfriends and apparently embarked on his killing spree following the loss of his job after an argument with a gay colleague. He was jailed in 1993 for murdering five men, each of whom he picked up in an Earls Court bar before returning to their homes where he smothered or strangled them. He also tortured a couple of his victims until they gave him their PIN numbers for their bank cash-cards. During the hunt for the killer, Ireland taunted police by phone. Finally, he claimed that he would stop after victim number five, saying 'I think it is for four people that the FBI classify as serial – so I am stopping now I have done five. I just wanted to see if it could be done.' However, police were not certain the man would have stopped at five. Fortunately, they tracked him down after he was seen on a security video with his final victim in Charing Cross Railway Station. He was imprisoned for life with the judge's recommendation that he never be freed.

Similarly, Italian-born fashion consultant Michele Lupo launched a two-month-long killing spree in 1986, murdering four men and trying to kill a further two when he discovered that he had contracted the HIV virus. The fact that he contracted the virus is not surprising, considering he once boasted of having had over 4,000 lovers during his sexual career – often having as many as four in a single night. He finally succumbed to illness in Durham Prison in February 1995, having refused medical treatment and painkillers.

But the most famous British homosexual killer is probably civil servant Dennis Nilsen, a Scot and one-time trainee police officer. His habit was to pick up sexual partners in Soho and take them to his flat in north-west London where he strangled them or held their heads under water in a basin. He killed 12 men in total, dismembering most of them and storing the body parts under floorboards in his first flat until they could be burned in garden fires. In a second flat, he cut up and boiled the bodies in a large pot and disposed of the resulting sludge down the toilet. He was eventually caught when a plumber, called to investigate blocked drains, found pieces of human flesh in the underground pipes.

Dismemberment played a crucial role in another Scottish case, although this time the man convicted of the murder more or less gave himself away by telling people the name of the victim . . .

BODY BAGS

It was just before New Year, 1992, and a police dog was being exercised on Law Hill – a stump of volcanic rock looming up over the jute city of Dundee – when it found the first body part. It was an arm, reaching out from a black plastic bag, lying among other bags in a bundle. The young girl in charge of the dog, the daughter of its handler, ran back home and informed her mother. And so began the Dundee Torso Murder case, described by the judge as a 'nauseating and barbaric murder'.

When police officers arrived to delicately sift through the bags, they found not only the forearm and hand but also part of a lower torso, thighs and upper torso with a section of the other arm still attached. A second batch of bags was discovered in the city's Dudhope Park and this time increasingly horrified searchers found other body parts, including a severed foot with a lady's stocking still attached to it.

But the head, along with other portions and organs, was still missing, making identification of the body all that more difficult. Not impossible, but difficult. They even took the unusual step of lifting the corpse's fingerprints from deep impressions on the left hand – the first time this had ever been done in Scotland – but there was no match on their files. Finally though, following a massive media appeal, police identified the corpse as that of Gordon Dunbar, a 53-year-old qualified architect who had only arrived in the east coast city three years before, after spending a number of years abroad working for the War Graves Commission and later running his own café in Paris. He had been living in a rooming-house in Victoria Road but had not been seen since Christmas Eve. Pathologists studying the remains found that the man had indulged in anal sex at some time before or after death.

Police believed that whoever did this terrible thing may have killed before and so their attention was drawn early on to 43-year-old Glasgow-born Alastair Thompson. In 1968, while only a teenager, Thompson was convicted of murdering his 74-year-old grandmother by stabbing her 16 times with a carving knife and beating her with a hammer. It was, apparently, the culmination of a litany of brutality which also included strangling a pet rabbit and snapping a cat's spine. He was sentenced to life but was released on licence in 1984, when he married a divorced prison visitor. The marriage failed after a year and Thompson moved to Dundee but was soon in trouble again, accused of slashing a man with a carpet knife. The charge was found Not Proven although his licence was revoked and he was returned to prison to do another three years, being released again in January 1992.

Thompson, it would seem, could not keep his mouth shut and had been discussing the torso murder hunt with friends. This, in itself, was nothing unusual – the macabre case was a favourite topic in many a pub at the time. But Thompson knew more than everyone else. He knew the victim's name and he would say to friends, 'Remember the name – Gordon Dunbar.' He also presented a female friend with a thick gold chain, later identified as belonging to the murdered man. But the real problem was the story he told another friend, who subsequently repeated it in court.

This man claimed that Thompson told him that he had been asked to dispose of a body as a favour for two lads from either Glasgow or Edinburgh. They were hit-men and they had murdered the man and then had cut up the corpse into pieces and left it in a bath. He said he planned to get rid of some of the parts on Law Hill, which was not very far away from the flat. He estimated it would take three or four trips to dump them all. But the head, he said, was in a skip in the Kirkton area of Dundee, although he did express a desire to mount it on a stake outside the city's Bell Street police headquarters. At the time, the man to whom Thompson told this could not decide whether to believe him. He thought perhaps Thompson was pulling his leg, which was, perhaps, not the most delicate way to put it under the circumstances.

Police searched Thompson's room in a hostel run by the prisoners' welfare society, SACRO – where he worked as a caretaker – and found a bloodstained shirt, bloodstained trousers and a T-shirt. They also discovered the keys to a flat in Butterburn Court.

And when they entered the flat, they realised it was the scene of the butchery.

According to the prosecution, Thompson had somehow lured his victim to the flat, which was owned by another friend staying in London who had told him to use it whenever he liked. Naturally, the man had not expected his flat to be used as a slaughterhouse. Once in the flat, it was alleged, Thompson stabbed the man twice, once fatally to the heart. And after that came the problem of disposal.

On Christmas Day, the Crown case went on, Thompson borrowed two hacksaws from an acquaintance on the pretext of sawing up some pipes. Back at Butterburn Court, he placed Dunbar's body in the bath and began the messy process of dismemberment. A pathologist would later testify that the bones of the body parts found showed that they had been sawed through. He also said that it would be relatively easy for someone to cut up a body, once that person had overcome his initial disgust and revulsion. Apparently, it is just like carving your Sunday joint or a large chicken. Once he had sliced the body up, Thompson placed the parts into some plastic bags which he had bought from a SPAR store and sealed them with masking tape. One by one, he placed the bags into a hold-all and carried them to the dumping places. He then cleaned the bathroom and other parts of the flat in the hope of covering up all traces of his bloodthirsty deed. But, like James Keenan, who in 1969 murdered then dismembered his wife and dumped the pieces across Central Scotland, Thompson did not realise that you cannot totally dispose of or conceal every single cell. Dismemberment may well be just like cutting up your roast, but a roast does not bleed copiously. When police experts tore the bathroom apart, they found traces of blood and human remains in the bath's drainage system, while further blood had seeped through the carpeting.

DNA profiling matched the blood found in the rug and on Thompson's shirt. His fingerprints were found on a tumbler in the flat. He had Mr Dunbar's gold chain. The people to whom he had talked were found and made statements. Masking tape found in his room was similar to that used on the bags. Unsurprisingly, Thompson was charged with murder. But the head, as well as other pieces of the body, still had not been found. If indeed it was in a skip, police assumed that it had either been incinerated along with the other items or had been discarded in a rubbish dump somewhere.

During his trial, Thompson insisted his story about the two hit-men was true. He admitted dismembering and disposing of the body, which he said he did in a panic, but denied emphatically that he had killed Gordon Dunbar. The jury, however, did not believe him and took only 70 minutes to find him guilty by unanimous vote.

Then in August 1993, he told a reporter from the *Scottish Sun* where a bag with further remains lay. The journalist had known Thompson for many years and he had continued to visit him in Perth Prison. One day, the prisoner told him he would find another

Part of Salisbury Crags in Edinburgh, showing the Radical Road. It was from these rocky cliffs that Helga Konrad plunged to her death

Robert Mone senior, who murdered three women to prove he was as dangerous as his son, the so-called Carstairs axeman (*The Scottish Sun*)

Noel Ruddle, who was commanded by voices to kill with a kalashnikov copy
(*The Scottish Sun*)

James Boyce, who gunned down a German tourist during a robbery near Stranraer and then attempted to kill the man's wife and two children (*The Scottish Sun*)

ABOVE: Bothwell Bank Sewage-works where Peter McMurray blasted three fellow workers to death in 1985 and then, in 1992, where the remains of George Hall were found (*The Scottish Sun*)

RIGHT: Sewage-workers at Bothwell Bank Sewage Plant show where George Hall's remains were found. The works had been the scene of an earlier tragedy in 1985 when a worker seemingly went berserk and blasted three colleagues to death (*The Scottish Sun*)

George Carlin who admitted luring victim George Hall to his death during the Body in the Sewer case. But who actually pulled the trigger? (*The Scottish Sun*)

Armed officers stay alert as Raymond McCourt is led from a house following the shootings in Cambuslang Main Street in 1993 (*The Scottish Sun*)

The Glasgow townhouse where assistant procurator fiscal Marshall Stormonth was brutally murdered (*The Scottish Sun*)

LEFT: Alastair Thompson, who admitted dismembering the body of Gordon Dunbar, but still insists he did not kill the man (*The Scottish Sun*)

BELOW: Police officers carefully remove a rotting plastic bag filled with human remains from a Dundee dump. The remains were part of Gordon Dunbar and the police were led there by *The Scottish Sun* after Alastair Thompson told a freelance reporter where to find them (*The Scottish Sun*)

bag at a certain spot, drawing a crude map on the back of a biscuit wrapper as a guide. The reporter decided to check out the claim before handing the map over to the police and drove to the location specified – a Dundee City Council depot. It was at the bottom of a bridge parapet that he first detected the sickly sweet smell of decay. There were plastic bags there but he could not get to them so he first went to Thompson's solicitor and then to the police.

Officers searched the area and found a bag containing further human remains, including parts of the spinal column and the rib cage. A more complete search by police revealed another two bags nearby. One had soiled clothing and towels while the other one may have held more organs and remains wrapped in paper – but at some time animals had chewed their way into the bag and taken them.

When he provided the location of these remains, Thompson had been hoping he was aiding an appeal. He continued to insist that he did not kill the man and told reporters that he fully intended to name the real culprit in court should he get another chance. He claimed that the murderer was a witness against him at his trial and had received immunity in return for testifying against Thompson. This man, Thompson alleged, helped him dump the body parts. He also claimed that the body he dismembered had no stab wounds on it.

So far though, he has not been able to have his case referred to the courts.

And the head has never been found.

Murder Chain

DEATH ON THE ROAD

IN APRIL 1961, a man absconded from Hartwood Mental Hospital in Lanarkshire. He had transferred there the previous July from another institution, where he had been a voluntary patient, having been finally certified insane by doctors.

He was recaptured some time later but, because of a curiosity in law, he was not required to return to the hospital. For even though he had been deemed a danger not just to himself but also the public, he had managed to remain at large for over 28 days without any trouble and so he was, effectively, cured.

But he was far from cured, as he proved two years later.

For the same man, suffering from terrifying religious delusions, killed two men in two separate incidents and would have carried on killing had he not been captured. He also forged the first link in a bizarre chain of events, mixing murder, madness and retribution which would ultimately claim the lives of ten people.

George Green had been looking forward to coming back to Scotland for his skiing holiday. He had previously toured the Highlands with his brother and he had been captivated by the country's rough beauty.

On 7 March 1962, the 30-year-old electrical engineer said good-bye to his mother in his Leeds home and climbed into his black Ford Anglia to begin the long journey north. His happiness at setting off on his journey would have been marred by the argument he'd had with his fiancée, Sheila, who should have been going on holiday with him. But that could be sorted out on his return. After all, most couples have arguments at some time or another.

Had Sheila gone with him on the trip as planned, then there is every possibility that George Green would be alive today. For somewhere on the road between Perth and Inverness he met the man who would murder him.

The A9 was then, as it is now, the main road northwards. However, in 1962 it was not the busy pseudo-motorway that we know today. Whereas nowadays great stretches of the A9 are dual carriageway, the road of 30-odd years ago was merely a two-lane highway with nowhere near as many cars roaring over its tarred surface. It wound its way north across some bleak and desolate countryside, skirting round the bases of heather-covered hills and over highland passes blocked regularly by winter blizzards.

These days, many drivers see the road as a deathtrap with high-powered vehicles zooming up and down it as if the national speed limit was a figment of a traffic cop's imagination, or playing a dangerous game of leap-frog by weaving round slower vehicles on those stretches that are still single-laned, dodging swiftly out of the path of oncoming traffic. But in 1962, it was a deathtrap for quite another reason.

Ian Simpson's plan was to kill someone on that road but he had not yet found the right person. He had a profile to follow – a blueprint for murder, it was later called. Driven by religious fervour, Simpson stalked the roadway like an avenging angel, looking for a suitable victim. He had already hitch-hiked the 100 miles from Perth to Inverness and back again without finding The One, but he was confident he would find him. He possessed the instrument of purification and God would lead him to the right person. It was all a matter of waiting.

As he headed for the ski slopes of the Cairngorms, George Green saw the figure standing at the side of the road with his thumb out and decided to be a good Samaritan. It was pretty cold outside and the ground was hard with frost. It could not be much fun hitching in this weather. Anyway, he was lonely and it would be nice to have someone to talk to on the final leg of his journey. He stopped the car and the man climbed in.

That kindly act sealed George Green's fate. From that moment on, it was only a matter of time.

The two men talked as the car moved steadily northwards. Simpson told the driver he was a theology lecturer at Manchester University. He seemed likeable and pleasant, and the two men got on well together – until the conversation turned to religion. They had a disagreement and there was a mild argument. Nothing violent, though. That would come later, for Simpson had found his victim. God had told him this was The One; a man who needed to be saved from his own sin, a soul to be purified.

At some point in the journey, Simpson drew out his .22 pistol and saved the holidaymaker's soul by shooting him in the head. He died instantly.

Simpson searched the body, stripping it of all means of identification, then drove the car to a lay-by three miles south of Newtonmore in Inverness-shire. There, as the darkness gathered swiftly in the Highland sky, he dumped the body in a small hollow beside a tree and covered it with earth and twigs. Then, with the dead man's wallet and £40 in cash in his pocket, he drove off south, believing his victim would not be discovered for some time yet.

Although a Scot – born and brought up in Coatbridge – 26-year-old Simpson was at that time living in Manchester, in lodgings on the Lancashire city's Hathersage Road. His landlady and other acquaintances thought he was a graduate of the University of Glasgow who gave evening lectures at Manchester University. What they did not know was that in actual fact he spent his evenings not discussing theology with students, but up to his elbows in dirty dishes in the city's Queen's Hotel.

The day after the murder, Simpson blatantly drove the stolen car into the yard behind the lodgings and, as his landlady watched from the kitchen window, began to clean it out. He was a nice man, was Mr Simpson, an ideal lodger really. Quiet, courteous and always willing to run an errand. Ever such a nice man.

Simpson lost no time in having the black car repainted, although he did a very poor job. He told people that it had belonged to a student who could not keep up the payments. And they believed him. He was such a decent sort, was Ian. So devout. He couldn't harm a fly . . .

Meanwhile, over a week later, Simpson's murderous handiwork had been discovered by water bailiff James Mathieson, a

101

former sergeant with the Metropolitan Police. The killer had not done as good a job at hiding the body as he had thought. The retired policeman literally stumbled on the body, catching sight of the foot sticking out from the mound of leaves and twigs, and then he saw the back of a head. He alerted the police who immediately launched a murder hunt.

The first thing they had to establish was the identity of the victim. A description was issued to the press – five foot eight-to-nine inches tall, between 25 and 35 years of age, wearing a grey-green anorak with no hood, high-necked jersey, white silk shirt with collar attached, green tie, white string-net undervest, clerical grey trousers, maroon socks and brown shoes – while detectives visited hotels, guest houses and hostels in the area, armed with a photograph of the dead man.

But the real break came from a crafty piece of detection. By studying the soles of his shoes they surmised that the man had driven quite a distance. The tread on the sole of the right shoe, although new, showed signs of wear, as if he had been pressing it on an accelerator. Also, they found a map of Leeds near where the body was found, with the address of a garage written on it.

Leeds police were asked to contact the garage and give the owner a description of the dead man to see if it sparked off a memory. It did. The garage owner was able to say that the dead man sounded like George Green, who was on holiday in Scotland. He told them he drove a black Ford Anglia, registration number YUM 772.

At the request of their Scottish counterparts, West Yorkshire officers visited the deceased's home in Leeds' Woodlee Street and spoke to his mother, whose worst fears had come true. She had been worried sick about her son, who had been due to return home from his holiday two days before. She agreed to make the heart-breaking trip to Inverness to officially identify the body.

So now police had a name for the murdered man and a description of the missing car – which was probably the most important lead in the case. In fact, it was the only lead. So far, their inquiries had only revealed that the man had perhaps been seen at the Craigdhu Transport Café, on the south side of Newtonmore, 47 miles from Inverness, on Tuesday or Wednesday of the previous week. So far, no one in any of the hotels and guest houses visited by police had recognised the photograph of the dead man, which meant that he had never reached his destination. Find the car, they reasoned, and they would find their killer.

An urgent nationwide appeal was made to trace the stolen vehicle. Police forces all over the country were alerted, with officers being told in no uncertain terms that should they find the Ford Anglia, under no circumstances were they to touch it, for fear of disturbing any fingerprint or other forensic evidence. AA patrols were asked to be on the lookout for the car and also questioned whether any of their patrols had actually seen it heading to or from Scotland round about 12 March. The investigating team was rewarded with dozens of sightings of a black Ford Anglia from all over Scotland and England – even as far as Wales – but none of them turned out to be the car they were looking for. Quarries, gullies, rivers, remote buildings and stretches of moorland were scoured for sign of it. But they found nothing, not even a tyre track.

Meanwhile, police officers – supported by 75 Territorial Army troops from the 45th Battalion Queen's Own Cameron Highlanders – were conducting an inch-by-inch search of the roadway and surrounding area between Newtonmore and Dalwhinnie for further clues. Metal detectors were brought in to help find the murder weapon, which they believed may have been discarded. But all they managed to uncover was a child's cap pistol, thick with dirt and rust.

The dead man's mother, Molly, had come to Scotland to identify the body, praying all the way that it was not her son lying in the Highland mortuary after all; that it was all a horrible mistake, that George was on his way home even while she was travelling north. That he was safe and well and alive.

But it was her son. And he had been murdered. And his killer was still on the loose.

As she returned home from Inverness, Mrs Green spoke to reporters. Her other son, David, held her hand as she spoke, tears never far from her voice. 'Someone, somewhere must be able to help,' she said. 'This killer could strike again. For all our sakes, I beg anyone with any information – no matter how slight – to come forward. George's car hasn't yet been found. It must be somewhere.'

Repeating words that have been said by countless mothers before and since, she continued, 'I will not rest until George's killer is found and brought to justice.'

She spoke about the argument her son had with his fiancée, saying that the fact that Sheila had not gone on the holiday was the only blessing in this sad story. Had she gone, the woman said, she might have been murdered, too. Sheila had already told reporters that the reason she did not go was that she could not ski, and a week was not long enough for her to learn. However, the dead man's mother insisted there had indeed been a row which had not been patched up. 'I don't think the engagement was broken off,' she said, 'but it was one of those fights young couples have. No doubt everything would have been settled when he returned. But he never got the chance . . .'

She said that she had begun to grow worried when there was no word from her son. He had promised to get in contact once he arrived, but there had not been a letter or a postcard from him. Her mind had turned to the A6 murder she had been reading so much about. You never think it could happen to you, she had thought, but here she was, with a son murdered . . .

The so-called A6 murder took place on 22 August 1961.

Married-man Michael Gregston and his lover, Valerie Storie, were in a car parked beside a field near Slough in Buckinghamshire when a man armed with a gun forced his way into the car and told them to drive to a lay-by just off the A6. There he shot Mr Gregston and raped and shot Ms Storie, leaving her for dead.

A man called James Hanratty was subsequently arrested and tried for the murder, although there were grave reservations over the quality of the evidence against him. To this day, there are doubts as to whether Hanratty really was the A6 murderer, although those doubts cannot do him much good now. The unfortunate man was hanged on 4 April 1962.

Mrs Green repeated that it was important that the public help find her son's killer, as there was every chance that he would kill again.

She was right.

While the search was on to find the car – by now repainted, with stolen number plates replacing the distinctive YUM 772 plates – Simpson was carrying on his life in Manchester. He had developed a relationship with a Warrington nurse – whom, he said in a love letter, fulfilled his 'ideal of womanhood' – and during this period he would visit her at her parents' home, daringly parking his car in the street outside in the full knowledge that three policemen lived opposite, thereby cocking a snook at the nationwide alert.

He had also struck up a friendship with 28-year-old van driver Arthur Shaw, who had commented on the fact that the car Simpson was driving could be the one the police were looking for. Simpson finally confirmed that it was, telling him that he had not purchased it from a hard-up student as he had originally claimed, but had actually found it abandoned in a Manchester street. But Simpson was a convincing storyteller and he managed to assure Shaw that he was not the killer, saying he could not approach the police as he feared they would arrest him for a crime he did not commit. Mr Shaw was with Simpson when he threw the original number plates in a Derbyshire reservoir and, later, the gun (which Simpson said he found in the car), into the River Mersey. Perhaps rather gullibly, Mr Shaw still believed Simpson's protestations of innocence. Later, he would come to regret it as he faced death at the man's hands on an icy rock face.

But before he disposed of the weapon, Simpson had another job to do.

Hans Rudi Gimmi was a 24-year-old visitor to Scotland. A student textile designer, he was staying in Edinburgh but was due to return to his home in Zurich to be best man at his sister's wedding on 14 April. Prior to that, he had intended taking a trip to the Highlands before attending a skiing conference in Inverness. He left his lodgings in Edinburgh on 8 April 1962 and never returned. Nor did he make it to Switzerland. The furthest he got was a lonely grave in a remote forest in Dumfriesshire.

At a youth hostel near Loch Duich in Wester Ross, Gimmi met up with the smiling theology lecturer from Manchester and struck up a friendship with him. The lecturer agreed to drive him south, calling first at Loch Lomond and then staying a night at Moffat in Dumfriesshire. The following day, they continued their journey, stopping to have a picnic in Twiglees Forest on Eskdalemuir. Here, 250 miles away from the site of his first killing and 15 miles from Lockerbie, Simpson felt the religious fervour build up inside him once more. God spoke to him again, whispering words of death. Here was another soul in need of redemption.

The pistol cracked sharply in the silence of the forest and Simpson had murdered for a second time. As the tall fir trees around him swayed and creaked in the breeze, he removed all identification and buried his new victim in a shallow grave and headed south once again. Only the trees and the birds and the wind knew what he had done. The young student's corpse would not be found until after his killer's arrest.

Again, Simpson went back to Manchester to resume his double life posing as a university lecturer but in reality making a living as a dishwasher. He must have been aware of the vast man-hunt being conducted in the Highlands and taken great pleasure out of knowing that there was another – as yet undiscovered – crime far to the south. Only he knew the truth, that the two men had not been killed but 'changed'; their souls purged of the moral darkness into which they had fallen.

But his friend Arthur also knew he had the car. Arthur might talk. Arthur was a danger to his work. Arthur would have to be taken care of.

The attempt was made on 22 April. Simpson and his new friend were in Wester Ross on a climbing holiday and the plan was to scale one of the area's many mountains. The pair set out early and Simpson selected an ice gully as a means up the chosen mountain. He started the ascent first, followed by Shaw.

About halfway up the slippery face of the gully, Shaw felt the rope around his waist began to jerk spasmodically. The rope supposedly linked him to his climbing partner above, but when Shaw looked up to shout a warning, he saw that it was not attached to Simpson, who was tugging at the end, his face gleaming with a strange light. Clinging to the ice, Shaw screamed at him to stop but Simpson just carried on seemingly trying to force him off the rock face. His fingers working desperately, Shaw managed to loosen the rope from his body just as Simpson 'gave a terrific tug' and the line snaked off into the gully below. Had he not managed to disentangle himself, he was in no doubt that he would have plummeted to his death.

Later, Simpson apologised, saying that there had been a mix-up, but Shaw still remembered the strange glint in his eyes. The incident reminded Shaw that Simpson had once said to him that the way to commit the perfect murder was to fake a mountaineering accident.

But still Simpson remained at large. That was about to change, however. At the beginning of the murder hunt, police had been aided by a garage owner in Leeds who helped them establish the dead man's identity. Now, the sharp-eyed son of a Manchester garage owner would lead them to the killer.

On Friday, 4 May 1962, Simpson drove the stolen car into a Manchester garage. The owner's 19-year-old son first noticed the very poor paint job on the car's bodywork and then his attention was drawn, more tellingly, to the number plates. In replacing the distinctive YUM 772 plates, Simpson had used plates from a 1949 model. The car he was driving was a 1957 model.

The young man was immediately suspicious and, when Simpson left the garage, followed and finally overtook him before driving to the nearest police station. Officers stopped Simpson and questioned him.

And then let him go.

It was not until the plates were checked against records that police realised they had stumbled on to something important and detectives raced around to Simpson's lodgings. They found him in his room, sitting on his bed eating an apple, his bags packed beside him. He had arrived with two suitcases, he now had seven. Most of the clothes were not his but were those of his victims. They also found the spade which was used to dig Hans Rudi Gimmi's grave and the dead man's ticket to Zurich.

After a seven-week search, Manchester police had caught the notorious A9 killer.

During an interview, 26-year-old Simpson told them about Gimmi's body, buried in the Eskdalemuir forest. On Sunday, 6 May, local police began a search and found the makeshift grave among the silent trees.

Simpson was brought back to Scotland the following week, arriving by car with his head covered by a coat. Two police officers bundled him from the back of the car and into Inverness Castle, where he took up overnight residence in a police cell. The following day, he was taken to a sheriff's room within the 250-year-old castle, his face again hidden from photographers' cameras and the eyes of the curious, where he was charged in private with the two murders and associated thefts. Then he was transported to Porterfield Prison, where he was to await trial.

In the subsequent three months, Simpson was studied by various psychiatrists, who diagnosed him as insane and therefore unfit to plead. They said he showed 'abnormal religious motivation', and had chosen victims who had not lived up to his peculiar moral standards. He was on a divine mission, he told them. God had told him to do it and he suggested that he would have continued in his work had he not been caught. One doctor noted that Simpson believed he really had achieved something by killing these two men; that the man felt he was doing these things to improve the people of the world. To Simpson, though, the men were not dead. They were merely 'changed'.

His mental state was probably best exemplified by a line from a letter he sent to his former girlfriend in Manchester while he was in prison in Inverness. He wrote, 'It is not really a matter of what we believe but how we translate our beliefs into action.'

Women, however, were safe from him. He did not involve himself in the fateful religious discussions with females, only men. But he did not murder without thinking. Once he had felt the urge to kill, the act was carefully planned and only committed when he knew he could make a clean escape.

Meanwhile, some old unsolved cases were being dusted down in police file rooms as officers checked to see if this holy terror could have been responsible. Among them was the mystery of 12-year-old Moira Anderson, who vanished from a Coatbridge street during a ferocious blizzard in 1957. Simpson, who came from Coatbridge, had been picked up for questioning by police three times during the initial investigation. Was it possible that he had, after all, murdered the young girl? But there was still no evidence and the disappearance of little Moira remained a mystery. However, in 1992, police did reopen the case following further information from a woman who claimed her father may have killed the youngster. However, despite gallant efforts, police were unable to make the allegation stand up and no arrest was made. (For a full account of this case, see *No Final Solution*, Mainstream, 1994.)

In August 1962, the psychiatrists laid their findings before the High Court of Edinburgh. As they outlined their diagnosis of Simpson's mental state, the short but well-built killer sat in the dock, his fleshy face occasionally grimacing at their remarks. He listened as his life story was paraded before the judge, Lord Kilbrandon, who heard that he had first got into trouble at the age of eight, when he set fire to a haystack near his home. At one time in his youth, he felt propelled to wash and take baths almost constantly. His mother said that he would have bathed every hour if he had been allowed. As he grew older, his moods would swing violently from elation to deep gloom and depression. He was also prone to sudden and violent fits of temper. As time went on, he developed criminal tendencies, stealing for no reason and giving what he stole away, while he seemed to live more and more in a fantasy world, claiming to be able to read minds. At various times, he had posed as a doctor, as the nephew of the Duchess of Windsor and as a minister – even attempting to form his own church. It was when he was caught stealing communion artefacts from a Dumfries church that he tried to kill himself in a police cell, winding up at Hartwood Hospital, having been diagnosed as insane and a public danger.

He absconded in 1961 and was eventually picked up again for theft, however, as we have already seen, because he had remained at large for over 28 days, he was officially deemed sane and sent to a mainstream prison. He was released again in January 1962 and four months later committed his first murder.

The legislation which allowed this to happen originated in the Lunacy (Scotland) Act of 1862 and subsequently enshrined in the Mental Health (Scotland) Act of 1960 and then again in the same Act of 1984. Lord Kilbrandon delivered some measured criticism of 'the system' which allowed a man who had been certified as a danger to the public to be returned to what he called 'the old routine' of prison life. After the trial, the killer's mother was more direct.

'If the law had been different,' she said, 'my son would never have had the chance to kill. He would have been where he belongs – in a mental home!'

And it was to just such an institution that Simpson was eventually sent. The judge declared he should be taken to the State Hospital at Carstairs where he was to be detained without limit of time.

It was there that the smiling, podgy killer – declared the most evil killer in Scotland since Peter Manuel – would meet his own murderers.

Soldier Robert Mone had been detained under Section 63 of the Mental Health (Scotland) Act 1960 and sent to Carstairs in January 1968. Two months before, he had forced his way into a Dundee primary school armed with a shotgun and, after two hours of terrorising the girls in a needlework class, shot to death their teacher, 26-year-old Nanette Hanson. Thanks to the bravery of student nurse Marion Young, with whom Mone had once been friendly and who agreed to go into the classroom and talk to the armed man, the young girls were eventually freed and Mone was arrested.

At Carstairs, Mone ultimately met and formed an unhealthy alliance with Thomas McCulloch, who on 16 May 1970 had shot and wounded two hotel employees in Erskine. He, too, was certified as insane and sent to Carstairs for treatment.

The two men plotted to escape from the hospital, and were, over a period of time, able to manufacture the lethal weapons which were to aid their bid. On Tuesday, 30 November 1976, they made their move, viciously attacking nursing officer Neil McLellan.

But they had not predicted that they would be opposed by another inmate – Ian Simpson. The former A9 killer had apparently flowered in the hospital, his intelligence blooming until he won himself a Bachelor of Arts degree through the Open University. He also displayed an aptitude for music, learning to play the guitar and teaching others. He could make and repair instruments. He was still a classic psychopath, though – charming and cunning – and it was unlikely he would ever have been released from care. However, it was his misfortune to be in the room when Mone and McCulloch made their bid for freedom.

Simpson was in an office talking to nursing officer McLellan while Mone and McCulloch were next door in the hospital's social club, where they were ostensibly recording books for illiterate patients. Suddenly, the two men burst in, spraying paint stripper at both Simpson and McLellan. Mone tackled the nursing officer while McCulloch drew a knife and went for his fellow patient, hacking at him. The viciousness of the attack stunned even Mone, who had planned the escape in the belief that they could get away without any fatalities. Mr McLellan seized Mone's momentary hesitation to leap to Simpson's aid, who was fighting fiercely, managing to wrest the knife from McCulloch's grasp.

The struggle spilled out into a hallway, with Simpson now fighting with Mone as McCulloch attacked McLellan with a home-made axe and then yet another knife. Mone finally hefted a garden fork, which was lying outside the office, and jabbed at Simpson, who collapsed to the floor, blood streaming from a number of wounds. McLellan also slumped to the ground, suffering from numerous wounds inflicted by McCulloch. The inmate then fell on top of the fallen man, still hacking and slashing with his weapon.

Mone and McCulloch left them bleeding on the hallway floor and went outside. Then McCulloch went back inside, found an axe in the office and chopped at both men until they were dead, severing Simpson's ears from his head in the process.

And so, Ian Simpson, the man who hid a psychotic desire to kill behind a cleric's dog-collar, died at the hands of a madman, trying to defend himself and a nursing officer. On Saturday, 4 November 1976, he was taken home to Coatbridge to be buried.

But Mone and McCulloch's night of terror was not yet over. They did manage to escape from the hospital compound and on a quiet stretch of road nearby they were approached by PC George Taylor as they attempted to hi-jack a passing motor car. McCulloch, his blood-lust now unstoppable, attacked and killed him. A second officer was also injured but managed to escape with his life.

The two killers then drove off in the officers' police car, which they later crashed into an embankment. They subsequently attacked two men in a van, bundled them into the back and – rather like their recent victim, Simpson, 15 years before – headed south. When they bogged the van down in a muddy field near Roberton in southern Lanarkshire, having taken fright at a railway light up ahead, thinking it was police, the men waded across the River Clyde (which is little more than a stream at that point), and forced their way into a farm. There they ripped the telephone from the wall and stole the farmer's car. But as they turned south again, they did not know that the farmer's daughter had managed to use an extension to alert the police.

At a roundabout near Carlisle, armed officers from the Cumbrian force rammed the stolen car and arrested the two men.

On 28 February 1977, they were sentenced to spend the rest of their lives in prison. Years before, Mone had been deemed insane and unfit to plead and so was sent to Carstairs. Now, along with

McCulloch, he had killed three more people and injured three others and yet, this time, he was to be sent to a mainstream prison. It would seem that by killing again they had proved themselves sane.

Meanwhile, PC Taylor's memory was honoured by colleagues with the unveiling of a plaque in Hamilton Police Station. Six years later, another plaque would be placed beneath it, in honour of Detective Sergeant Ross Hunt. (For a more detailed account of Mone and McCulloch's break-out, see *Blood on the Thistle*, Mainstream, 1992.)

But the murder chain does not end there and for the next link we must travel to the banks of the silvery Tay.

LIKE SON, LIKE FATHER

Catherine Millar disappeared from her Dundee home just before New Year 1979. The 29-year-old woman, who had only been married for five days, left her flat on 29 December to go to the bank and then to the shops. At half past four that day, she phoned her husband, John, to tell him she would be home in half an hour, telling him she was bringing home potatoes and asking him to get the steak on for their tea.

It was the last time her new husband would talk to her.

On the same day, a woman had disappeared from the Gray Memorial block of flats in Kingshorne Road, Dundee. This was a home for single women living on a strict budget, donated to the council by a local couple in memory of their parents. The area around the flats was known as No Man's Land because it was mainly populated by females. When 78-year-old Miss Agnes Waugh disappeared from her bed-sit in the block, it was at first believed that she was simply away visiting relatives for New Year. The elderly lady had been house-bound for some time following a fall in the street which had left her with an injured leg. But on New Year's morning the District Nurse called at her flat and, finding it empty, the alarm was raised.

Meanwhile, John Millar was trudging through snow-covered streets looking for his wife. He had informed the police, but because there is very little they can do when the missing person is a young, fit adult, he knocked on doors himself, asking if the occupants had seen her. He called at shops and banks and public houses – for, he admitted, both he and his wife had once had a drinking problem and had, in fact, met at a clinic. Through a friend he learned that his wife often voluntarily cleaned the flat of a Mrs Jean Simpson who lived in the block of flats in Kingshorne Road. Mr Millar hammered at the door of flat 2B but there was no reply so he went away again. He returned more than once over the next few days but did not manage to rouse anyone inside.

Meanwhile, the search for the elderly Agnes Waugh was continuing apace. Police officers and volunteers took to the streets while tracker dogs were also seen padding about in the snow, poking in building sites and sniffing across tundra-like parks and open spaces. Every one of the 24 flats in the block was to be searched and officers had already tried to get into Mrs Simpson's ground-floor bed-sit. Finally, on Thursday, 4 January 1979, two plainclothes officers involved in the search called again at Mrs Simpson's door. Like their colleagues and Mr Millar before them, the detectives received no reply and decided to go outside and look through a window. They had no reason to be suspicious, they were merely being thorough. They went to the back of the building and found a window lying open. They pulled back the curtains and peered into the bed-sit.

They could see the room and a recess bed – and a hand and arm dangling from the bed. It looked like a woman's hand. They called for help and the door was forced open. Inside, the officers found the tiny flat had become a death chamber.

The three women had been beaten and then strangled with stockings. Jean Simpson and Agnes Waugh were sitting on chairs by the fire, their wrists tied to the arms by plastic bags. Catherine Millar was on the bed, a flex from a radio also tightened around her neck. It was a horrible, tragic and frightening end to the search.

And for John Millar, still hoping his wife was all right, the shock of finding the flats sealed off by police officers was enormous. He was taken to a police station to make a statement regarding his wife's movements.

Police set up a caravan in the street to act as the murder incident room as door-to-door inquiries were carried out not only in the block of flats but also in other houses in the area. There seemed to be no apparent reason for the brutal triple killing, but from signs within the murder flat, investigating officers realised that the three women had been enjoying a party. As there was no indication of forced entry, it was possible that they knew the killer.

Within a day of the gruesome discovery, police issued descriptions of three men with whom they wished to talk. Two of them were in their fifties, one had stained teeth, the other had a broken nose while the third was in his twenties with a curly moustache. The men had been seen in the area between 29 December and 4 January. They also believed that a pair of candlesticks had been stolen from the flat and issued a description of them to the media.

But their inquiries were zeroing in on one man, 52-year-old Robert Mone – the father of the Carstairs killer. Mone senior was also Miss Waugh's half-nephew.

Police had found witnesses in a local pub – the Vennel in the city's Hilltown – who could testify that he had been in there on 29 December, boasting about being the father of one of the Carstairs axemen and vowing to make his own name just as famous – or notorious – as his son's. He wanted to show that he was, in fact, the old block from which the chip came. One witness said that Mone seemed to get into an argument with another drinker and later confided that the young man with whom he was fighting was 'going to have him before the night was out'. However, he also said, 'My son is a murderer. I have nothing to be frightened about.'

Mone's companion that day – and the man with whom he was apparently arguing – was 21-year-old Stephen Houston (not his real name), who said he met the older man in a bar and the pair of them then embarked on a day-long pub crawl around the town, ending at the Vennel. They had been drinking extensively and Mone was shouting, dancing and singing when they left at afternoon closing-time (this was before pubs in Scotland were granted all-day licences), armed with a carry-out. Houston said that Mone told him he had an aunt who lived nearby in Kingshorne Road and they could go there to drink.

They went to the block of flats but did not go to Agnes Waugh's flat. For some reason, Mone decided to knock on the door of 2B – Jean Simpson's flat – whom he also knew. A young woman opened the door to them; she turned out to be Catherine Millar.

Mrs Simpson invited them all into her flat for a New Year drink. However, Houston said he was feeling increasingly uncomfortable in the flat, especially as Mone had, apparently, made a homosexual pass at him. Eventually, Mone gave him cash to go to an off-licence and buy a half bottle of whisky, but Houston went to a bookie's instead, bet the money on a greyhound race and won himself eight pounds. He then went home, not wishing to return to that flat and block more advances from Mone. He insisted that Mrs Waugh was not in the flat when he left.

The police interviewed Mone, who, at this point, was being treated merely as a witness. He admitted he had been in the flat with the three women, but insisted they were all right when he left. Later, his defence would try to suggest that Mone had gone to buy the whisky, leaving Houston with the women.

During his police interview, Mone made a voluntary statement, saying, 'I have told you already, I have things to sort out, personal things. Once I have seen to them, I will make a statement that will tell you all you want to know.'

He said that there were only two people who loved him, his 14-year-old daughter Rose and 'him in Perth' – meaning his son, Robert. 'I visit him but there's a glass partition between us and two screws. I can't touch him,' the 'proud' father went on. 'All I live for is to be there beside him. If I was in there, I would see that he gets everything that's going – pills, booze, anything; the lot.'

At that time, police had little to hold him on, but inquiries continued and eventually, on 8 January, a warrant was issued for his arrest. When cautioned and charged with the three murders, Mone merely replied, 'You have my story. I stick to that.' He said no more.

Police had found fingerprints on a beer can at the scene of the murder which matched Mone's. Miss Waugh also had a distinctive wound on her cheek which may have been caused by a silver ring with a jade stone sometimes worn by Mone. The ring had actually been among his son's personal effects and was sent to him from Carstairs. Once recovered after the Dundee murders, it was analysed and found to bear traces of blood which could have come from Miss Waugh or Mrs Millar.

Mone's daughter, Rose, was called to give evidence against her father regarding this ring. When she stepped into the witness box, she burst into tears and was too hysterical to take the oath. Her father, who up until then had kept up an emotionless façade, finally erupted, rising up in the dock and snapping at the girl to 'Shut up!'. The teenager had to be taken away from the court to calm down but did finally return and said that her father had once given her the ring, telling her it would be useful in a fight.

However, a defence pathologist disagreed with the Crown that the ring could have caused the mark on Miss Waugh's face, while Mone's mother said that particular item of jewellery was in a drawer in her house on the day of the murders.

The ring was not the only thing that Robert 'Sonny' Mone shared with his son. He had been diagnosed as a psychopath in 1960, when he was jailed for five years for assault and robbery. The psychiatrist said then that it was his opinion that the man would never improve. He had been in trouble with the law since he was 16, when he was convicted of theft. That was in 1941, and the following year he was up on a serious assault and sodomy charge; while two years after that he was sent to borstal for theft. When he was released in 1946, he enlisted with the Black Watch but his military career was cut short three months later when he was thrown out for insubordination. He had also been arrested on a number of Breach of the Peace charges since 1967, when he would drunkenly and loudly proclaim his great pride in his son's murderous actions.

He also shared with his boy a fascination with Nazism and black magic – two interests which can often go hand-in-hand – and had the letters IHS tattooed on his chest, standing for 'In His Service', meaning the devil's. Another tattoo read 'I walk where angels fear to tread' while his left hand bore the print of a swastika. When young Robert was first arrested in 1967, Mone senior had told police that the boy had become part of a devil cult while he was serving with the Gordon Highlanders in Germany. He claimed his son had said, 'I've given myself body and soul to the devil. I've vowed to spill blood before I was 21.' Young Robert went on to kill Mrs Hanson in her classroom. He was 19 years of age. (The Army's special investigation branch investigated the death cult claims but could find no trace of it.)

Mone was not the most popular of men in Dundee. His unnatural pride in Mone junior's killings and his own sexual diversity alienated many around him. His first wife divorced him and his second wife had very little to do with him. When arrested for the murders, Mone refused to submit to a psychiatric evaluation, for fear that he would be found insane and unfit to plead and so be sent to Carstairs and not to Perth where he could be beside his son. While he seemed to have an affection for the boy which slid dangerously into the area of obsession, Mone senior was jealous of his son's 'achievements'. He wanted to be with him, while at the same time he wanted to outdo him. He became obsessed with committing murder, of showing the world – and his son – that he was just as dangerous as his offspring. That was why he had killed those three women in such a frenzy, beating them before strangling them.

When he came to trial in June 1979, he was also charged with various other offences, including the indecent assault of a 60-year-old woman a fortnight before the murders. The woman said that Mone had abducted her, beat her and threatened to kill her, and she described how she had been walking to a friend's house from a pub when Mone forced her into a taxi. He had been drinking heavily, she said, and told her he was taking her to his council house for a drink.

However, once they got into the house, she said that Mone had snarled at her, 'I've not brought you up here for nothing. I've brought you up here to kill you.'

The woman did not want to stay in the house but she said Mone had locked the door behind him and then, without warning, he punched her with such force that he broke her false teeth. She said he forced her to get into bed with him and another man and then he wrenched off her trousers. However, he could not get her jersey and waistcoat off.

The next morning he let her go, saying, 'If you shout "police" out there, you're dead.' She left the house with the warning ringing in her ears.

The man named in this *ménage à trois* confirmed that the woman had been struck on the mouth. He said he had gone into the kitchen to make some coffee and came back to find her bleeding. He also said that Mone forced him to climb into bed with him and the woman at the point of a knife.

The jury of 12 men and three women took just over 70 minutes to find Mone Guilty. He was sentenced to life in prison, with the judge's recommendation that he serve at least 15 years. As he was led from the dock, the man cursed and struggled with his escort, snarling 'Get your fucking hands off me,' and then shouting at the judge, 'Can't you back-date it?'

He did in fact get his long-cherished wish – he was sent to Perth Prison where his son was being held. But the authorities assured the public that he would be unlikely to see young Robert. He would be kept there only until the result of his appeal was announced and then, if that appeal was, in fact, refused, they would then decide where to send him. Finally – predictably – his appeal was refused and Mone was sent to Craiginch Prison in Aberdeen.

And it was there that the final link in the chain was bloodily hammered into place eight years later.

Even in prison, Mone liked to think of himself as a big man. He began to call himself 'Capone' Mone and swagger about the halls as if he owned them, threatening, according to one prisoner, that 'there will be a few bodies lying about this place' if he was not successful in a new appeal. To other inmates he was a bullying pervert who liked to prey on the younger men who were sent to do time. He was not liked by many inmates, whom he tried to rule, and in the end he was killed by one who could take it no longer.

Anthony 'Popeye' Currie, so called because he only has one eye, said that Mone was 'the personification of evil'. 'He was probably the most obnoxious man in the country, I mean that,' he said.

The prosecution tried to prove that 39-year-old Currie, who was doing time for armed robbery and assault, had embarked on a personal crusade against sex offenders, pointing out that in 1981 he had taken a chair leg to a child-torturer after the man commented that he would like to burn a child who had just appeared on television. It is not uncommon for 'straight' criminals to detest the men they call 'beasts' – the child and sex offenders who, more often than not, are placed on immediate protection by the prison authorities. However, it became clear that the killing of 'Sonny' Mone formed the climax to over a year of hate and persecution. Witnesses said that Mone abused Currie at every possible opportunity and on one occasion entered Currie's cell, dragged the man from his bed and threatened him with a piece of wood with a nail sticking out of the end. When another prisoner saw Currie later, he found the man allegedly 'shaking like a leaf' with the colour drained from his face.

Later, that prisoner was accosted by a knife-wielding Mone who demanded to know where he stood in the feud between him and Currie. The prisoner said it was nothing to do with him but advised Mone to make his peace with Popeye. Mone shook his head, the knife still in his hand, and said, 'No way is any peace going to be made. Currie will not be leaving the shed this morning.' Another witness said that he was in the toilet having a cigarette when Mone vowed that Currie would 'cop his whack before today is out'. As it turned out, it was Mone who copped his whack.

Prison officers said they knew nothing of Mone bullying Currie or other prisoners, but then they probably would not. Self-respecting inmates do not run to the 'screws', they take care of such matters in their own way. It happened during a teabreak and Mone was in the prison's main workshop collecting empty urns. At one point in his duties, he stopped to talk to another prisoner. It was then, according to a prison officer who was present, that Currie let out a cry which was somewhere between a roar and a scream, and launched himself at Mone, stabbing him from behind and then burying a knife deep into his neck, holding the blade there as the man slid to the ground, spitting out, 'At last, you perverted bastard, it's taken me 13 months but I've got you.'

The prison officer grabbed hold of Currie as Mone was rushed off to the surgery. A few minutes later, Currie was escorted past the room where a doctor was trying to save Mone and he shouted through the open door, 'I hope you die, you fucking old bastard.'

Mone had been stabbed nine times, including the neck wound and another through the heart. Currie pleaded self-defence, saying that Mone had come at him first with a knife. He admitted he had a knife with him, which he used to protect himself, before finally taking Mone's weapon away from him and holding a blade at the older man's throat.

'He saw the knife but he butted me on the nose,' said Currie, 'impaling himself on the knife. His eyes were open all the time as the knife was sliding in, he was glaring at me.'

But according to a prison officer who gave evidence, Currie said that he had actually been after two other inmates, both friends of Mone. However, the officer claimed, Currie thought Mone was 'a good compromise'.

Currie had been charged with Mone's murder but the jury reduced the charge to one of culpable homicide, believing that the man acted under provocation. They found him unanimously Guilty of this reduced charge and the judge sentenced him to a further eight years.

And so the death chain came to an end. It had stretched over 25 years and across the country; from Inverness-shire, to Dumfriesshire and then back up to the north-east, taking in Lanarkshire and Dundee on the way. A total of ten people died as each link was forged, including two of the 'blacksmiths'.

Visitors

DOUBLE INDEMNITY

ON THE MORNING of 14 October 1972, Herr Helmut Konrad, a wealthy businessman and farmer in what was then West Germany, received a telephone call from a young man in Edinburgh with some very disturbing news.

The young man identified himself as Ernst Dumoulin and before he could say much more, Herr Konrad demanded to know the whereabouts of his daughter, Helga. The 18-year-old girl had disappeared with this young man one month before and he and his wife had been worried to distraction ever since.

'We are married,' Dumoulin informed him, then asked, 'Can I call you father-in-law?'

'Where is Helga?' The worried father asked again.

'She is in Heaven,' the young man stated simply.

The father could not believe what he was being told. 'What happened?' he asked.

'An accident,' said Dumoulin across the telephone line and thousands of miles. Herr Konrad thought he might have heard a slight sigh in the voice, perhaps even the faint watery echo of tears, but he knew the young man to be something of an actor and he thought it might be put on. Then Dumoulin went on, 'Helga is dead.'

He did not tell the shocked father what sort of accident had apparently claimed the life of his daughter, although he did say he was thinking of committing suicide. Herr Konrad made immediate plans to travel to Edinburgh to find out what had happened. At the

121

back of his mind was the thought – perhaps the hope – that the young man was lying, that this was all some sort of elaborate scheme to chisel cash from him.

However, when he reached Scotland's capital he found out that his daughter was indeed dead; the victim in what is perhaps one of the strangest murder cases the small country has seen in modern times.

Things had not been going so well for 21-year-old Ernst Dumoulin. Born in Minden, West Germany, he had moved with his family at the age of one to Rotterdam. Later, his family returned to West Germany, although the boy was technically a Dutch National.

But things were not happy in the Dumoulin household. According to what was said in court later, his mother and father argued bitterly and eventually Ernst's older brother left home to make his own way. Ernst soon followed, studying commerce and banking. His brother, meanwhile, had established himself in a successful career in financial management and was earning the German equivalent of £1,000 a month. Ernst was ambitious – according to his boss at the time, he wanted to be a bank manager at 21 and a managing director at 30 – and tried to emulate his brother as best he could, but found that everything he touched turned to dust. By the spring and summer of 1972 his young life was in a turmoil. His work with a West German bank was not proving satisfactory and they would not be picking up his contract after his three-month probationary period. He was in debt to the bank to the tune of the German equivalent of £860 – a tidy sum in the early 1970s. And, to top it all, his fiancée had broken off their engagement. In June 1972, loneliness and desperation drove him to advertise in a newspaper.

Young man, 21, lacking other opportunities, seeks to meet a nice girl with a view to marry.

The advertisement was read by 18-year-old Helga Irmhild Konrad, who lived with her parents on their 60-acre farm near Schwerbel, a tiny hamlet consisting of a handful of houses and around 50 inhabitants. She responded to the newspaper plea and the two young people met. Helga was, quite literally, swept off her feet by the handsome 'financial consultant' and in early July she brought him to the farm to meet her parents.

Her father was unimpressed by this flash young man and when, eight days after first meeting him, Dumoulin dutifully came to him and asked for Helga's hand in marriage, the forthright farmer was less than complimentary. He did not trust Dumoulin; he did not believe he was able to support his daughter and he said to him, 'You're mad. Either that or you are joking.'

Although the young man appeared to be successful, Herr Konrad was suspicious of him. He had spoken about buying a flat, but Herr Konrad was not sure where the money was coming from. The farmer was chairman of a local bank and Dumoulin had once asked him of the possibility of a job there, but Herr Konrad said that was out of the question.

But Helga had fallen head over heels in love with this man whom she hardly knew. Her parents tried to convince her to wait before rushing headlong into matrimony, but she had her mind set. She was going to marry Ernst and that was it. However, she apparently acquiesced and seemed to settle down to wait.

But she and Ernst had hatched a plan to elope, and on 15 September 1972 they put that plan into action.

On that day, Ernst arrived at the farm in a new red Fiat 850 Sports Coupé – financed, as it turned out, by selling a car he did not own and also signing a dud cheque – and invited Helga out for a drive. Helga asked her father's permission to go driving for 'just 15 minutes' and he gave his grudging permission, saying, 'Don't be longer. We're busy here.'

The girl jumped into the sports car and waved to her father as Ernst steered it out of the farmyard. It was the last time Helmut Konrad would see his daughter alive.

When she failed to return that day, the farmer and his workers made a search of the surrounding area. Then he and his wife looked in Helga's bedroom and found her suitcase and some clothing were gone. He reported the teenager missing immediately – but a month would pass before he had any news, and when it came it was to tell him that his daughter was dead.

During that time, Ernst and Helga had fled across the continent; first to Paris, where they sold the car to buy tickets for America. But their attempts to reach the land of milk and money were stymied when Helga could not obtain a visa, so they opted for Britain instead, finally arriving in Edinburgh on 19 September, and taking up residence in a boarding house in Torphichen Street. The owner, 61-year-old Henry Wood, formed the opinion that the young couple were not married but fully intended to be, once they had fulfilled the 15-day residency requirement under Scottish law. Mr Wood gave them a room with two single beds. They later told him that Ernst intended setting up in business as a financial adviser, with his young wife as his secretary. Dumoulin had claimed that he already had three clients with large sums of money for him to invest.

But, like much of what Dumoulin told people, this was a fantasy. There were no clients, no large sums of money. There was nothing.

In Edinburgh, Dumoulin apparently set in motion a chain of curious financial dealings with a number of financial institutions. He called at the Bank of Nova Scotia and deposited £250 in a newly opened account. He also spoke to the manager, asking about the possibility of a £10,000 loan to buy a house. Dumoulin explained that the bank would have the house as security against the loan, as well as some fictional investments in Germany. He also said he wanted to open an employment agency for continentals coming to Scotland for work.

However, when the manager asked him for references – a common enough request, after all, and one that a so-called financial consultant would expect – Dumoulin hesitated and told the man he would have to think about it. The manager asked him to come back in two weeks, but never saw Dumoulin again. At least, not in his office.

In the meantime, Dumoulin had approached the Scottish Life Assurance Company with a proposal to insure he and Helga for £100,000 each in the event of accidental death. The company rejected the proposed policy, but it was suggested to Dumoulin that he see a chartered accountant, who in turn put him in touch with a representative of the Hambro Life Assurance Company.

It was on Thursday, 28 September, that William Syer, a sales associate with the insurance company, met with Ernst and Helga in the Caledonian Hotel. What Dumoulin was looking at, he explained, were two policies which would give £206,000 cover for

Helga and a similar amount for himself. Dumoulin also wanted to know if it was possible to arrange double cover in case of accidental death – the famous Double Indemnity clause. The insurance man said this would mean premiums of £200 per month for Helga plus £22.67 for the double cover, and £200 per month for Ernst plus £20.96. Ernst Dumoulin said this was fine but the salesman reminded him this was a great deal of money to pay out month after month. However, Dumoulin appeared unconcerned. He said he had money coming from Germany that would more than cover it.

However, he could not pay all of the first month's premium right away. He was still waiting for funds to be transferred, so would half now be satisfactory? The sales representative agreed and he went with the young German to the Bank of Nova Scotia where £221.85 pence was withdrawn from the recently opened account. The remainder would be paid when the money was transferred from Germany on 16 October. The amount paid would cover them for half the full amount for the month of October.

The salesman warned Dumoulin that should anything happen to either of them prior to the wedding, then any money payable would not go to the surviving partner but to the next of kin. Dumoulin said this was not a problem as he did not wish the policies to begin before they were married.

The applications were made on the understanding that they were still to be accepted by the company. If the company rejected them – as Scottish Life Assurance had already done – then the money already paid would be returned.

The problem was, there were no German investments and no funds being transferred on the sixteenth, unless Dumoulin had hoped Helga's father would send them money once he learned that his only daughter had married. Dumoulin did not even have a job in Scotland, although the couple did apply for, and were offered, posts as waiter and chambermaid in the Adelphi Hotel. But, even living in, these jobs would not pay anywhere near enough to cover the cost of the insurance premiums. In the end, neither Ernst or Helga took up the positions. Events overtook them somewhat.

On Friday 13 October, Ernst Bernhard Heinrich Dumoulin and Helga Irmhild Konrad were married in the registry office in Edinburgh's Haymarket. Their landlord, Henry Wood, and his wife acted as witnesses, afterwards treating the couple to a celebratory lunch and drinks in a Shandwick Place restaurant. Mr Wood later recalled that Ernst had three small whiskies while his new wife did not appear to drink any alcohol at all. Afterwards, Mrs Wood felt unwell and the older couple left the newly weds alone. Later that afternoon, Ernst and Helga returned to the boarding-house for a short time and then, at around 3.30 p.m., they went out for a walk.

What actually happened between then and 8.00 p.m. that evening can only be guessed. But it was certainly a Black Friday for Helga and her family.

At around 8.00 p.m. that night, a Mr and Mrs Crane were driving through Holyrood Park when they were stopped by a young man running towards them, waving his arms wildly and screaming, 'Ambulance! Ambulance! My wife has fallen!' Mr Crane swiftly turned his car around and drove back to his daughter's home in Royal Park Terrace, a residential street bordering the park, where his wife telephoned the police to report an accident while he and his daughter doubled back to the park armed with torches, blankets and towels. They searched the hillside, shouting for the man, their torches blinking in the darkness. But they could find no trace of him. Finally, though, as they walked up a path known as the Radical Road which skirts the steep cliffs leading to Arthur's Seat, they came across a group of police and civilians. An officer asked them what they were doing and when they told him, he asked them to go back down the hillside and go to the police office. As they reached the bottom of the crags, they saw the young man who had stopped the car being taken into a police car. He was still hysterical and they could hear him asking in his accented English, 'Can't you tell me what has happened?'

Two police officers had responded to Mrs Crane's call and had sped to the park, where they met a man who would contribute one of the puzzling facets of the case. The man gave his name as George Russell, claimed to be a merchant seaman and gave an address in South Lorne Place. This man took the officers to the spot on Radical Road where Helga lay dead. Later, he disappeared into the night and was never seen or heard from again; when police checked the address he gave they could find no trace of him.

Another puzzling, perhaps even sinister, event took place soon after the police arrived at the scene. Looking up the steep face of the rocky cliff, one of the officers thought he spotted a shadowy figure looking down at them from the top. The officers shouted and flashed their torches at the figure, but it just ducked back from the edge without answering. Of course, both the mysterious sailor and the shadow on the cliff top may just have been people who did not wish to involve themselves, but their brief appearance in the drama does add a certain frisson to the entire affair.

Dumoulin was finally found by officers after he had related his tale to another motorist, this time in the carpark adjacent to Holyrood Palace. He was then taken away in the police car, as witnessed by Mr Crane and his daughter. According to a police officer who spoke to him during this period, he did not seem to know that his wife was dead. The officer mentioned this to a member of CID who told him, 'Well, don't tell him just now.'

For while it was obvious that somehow Dumoulin's wife of just over ten hours had somehow tumbled to her death over the rocky escarpment, there were still questions to be asked; the most pressing being, did she fall – or was she pushed?

At around 3.00 a.m. on Saturday, 14 October, Henry Wood and his wife were roughly awakened from their sleep by someone banging on their door. Mr Wood went downstairs and found young Ernst standing on the doorstep of the boarding-house, his arm bandaged and his clothes caked with mud, as if he had fallen somewhere and had been rolling in dirt. The young man was accompanied by two Edinburgh detectives, who told the shocked landlord that Helga was dead. Ernst, the man recalled later, did not say a word. The detectives left Dumoulin in the boarding-house, after requesting that he return to Central Police Office along with Mr and Mrs Wood later that day.

That night, as they lay in bed discussing the shocking news, Mrs Wood suggested to her husband that he go into Ernst's room and turn off the gas fire. He presumed the precaution was in case the young man became so distraught over his wife's death that he would try to gas himself. After all, the young girl had died tragically on their wedding night.

But Dumoulin did not attempt to take his own life and the following morning the three of them went to the police office as requested. Police interviewed Ernst for three hours before finally releasing him again. When he returned to the boarding-house in

Torphichen Street once more, Ernst asked Mr Wood if he could play some of the records he and Helga had brought with them from Germany. Mr Wood said he heard the young man play one record over and over again – the theme to the film *Love Story*. He played the record very quietly so that he did not disturb anyone, but Mr Wood sensed that the song had some sentimental meaning to the man. After he had listened to the record, Ernst Dumoulin walked out again. All he had said to the Edinburgh couple regarding the death was, 'Why don't people take my word for it?'

That was the day that Ernst Dumoulin made his phone call to Helga's father in Germany.

The following day, 15 October, Dumoulin met with Mr Syer from Hambro again, this time in the Grosvenor Hotel, and told him what had happened. He said he and Helga had gone for a walk in the park in the evening and had sat down two metres from the edge of Salisbury Crags. There is a fine view from this point in the park, which could be called the roof of the city. From here you can see right over Scotland's capital, from the magnificence of Holyrood Palace to the folly of Calton Hill. You can look over the medieval old town to the New Town. Then there is the dark mass of Edinburgh Castle at the top of the Royal Mile, sitting on the plug of volcanic rock like some form of fortified growth. And beyond the patchwork quilt of roofs there is the wide expanse of the River Forth, with Fife shining brightly on the other side. As you sit there, high above the bluster of the modern-day city, feeling the wind caressing your face and breathing through the long grass all around, you can practically smell Scotland's history.

After a while, Dumoulin told the insurance man, his wife got to her feet suddenly, then somehow stumbled and plummeted over the cliff. The police had already interviewed him about the incident but 'they trusted him and had let him go.'

Dumoulin seemed to be of the firm opinion that the insurance company would not pay the amount due, because Helga had met her death on a mountain – the policy had a clause which prevented payment if death occurred during 'hazardous pursuits' like mountaineering. What Dumoulin did not seem to realise was that, although Salisbury Crags could be called mountainous, it is far from being a mountain, with the walk around Arthur's Seat being a favourite among Edinburgh citizens.

However, the insurance representative did not have the heart to tell him that there would be no pay-out anyway. The policy had not yet been processed and so the application had not been accepted. It was highly unlikely that the company would be paying anything.

Dumoulin went on to say that he had not told the police anything about the insurance policies. If he did make a claim, and it was settled, would this be made public? The insurance man told him that it would indeed. Dumoulin thought about this and then wondered if the proposal forms could just be destroyed.

But the proposal forms could not be destroyed, and the Hambro representative reported the conversation back to his employers, who subsequently informed the police of the matter.

Meanwhile, Helmut Konrad, who had arrived in Scotland, was given the sad news by police that his daughter was indeed dead. He met up with Dumoulin in a police station. The young man put his hand out towards his father-in-law but was met by an icy stare. The older man told him to try to be honest for once in his life and tell him what had happened to his daughter.

'It was an accident,' Dumoulin insisted. 'She fell down a mountain.'

But the German businessman was far from satisfied with this explanation. His mistrust of Dumoulin bubbled to the surface and he accused the young man of murder. 'You selected the highest place,' he said, 'and pushed her down.'

Two days later, Dumoulin wrote the grieving father a letter from his prison cell, saying, 'I sit here accused of having murdered my wife, Helga. Because Helga was your only child her death must hurt you terribly hard.

'Up to now my life has been full of misfortune but I still intended only the best. I would now like to express my sincere sympathy with you in the tragic death of your daughter.

'I must also emphasise that at all times I considered Helga my wife. I accept you never want to see me again. I am not a murderer.'

But Herr Konrad thought differently, and perhaps more importantly, so did the police and procurator fiscal. On Monday, 16 October, Dumoulin was arrested for the murder of his wife Helga. Police say that, after caution, he stated, 'I pushed my wife so that she fell down the cliff. I did not want to murder her or gain money.'

129

But later, during his trial, he would tell a fuller story which – had it been true – would have painted a different picture of Helga Konrad than that of an innocent young girl overawed by Dumoulin's good looks and flashy ambitions. According to Dumoulin, the girl was a calculating and ultimately homicidal young woman whose plan to kill her husband backfired.

The ten-day trial began on Tuesday, 23 January 1973, in the High Court of Edinburgh before Lord Wheatley and a jury of eight women and seven men. Every witness called – apart from one – was for the prosecution. The only defence witness was Dumoulin himself.

The crux of the prosecution case was that Dumoulin had attempted to take out these insurance policies for incredible sums while not actually having a regular source of income to pay the premiums. Or any source of income for that matter. He then pushed Helga from the top of Salisbury Crags in order to claim the money.

His earlier explanation for the death – that Helga had slipped from the crags – was refuted by Dr Robert Nagle, lecturer in forensic science at Edinburgh University, who had studied and measured the 96-foot cliff-face while dangling from the edge of a rope and communicating by radio with a colleague at the top. He was no stranger to this kind of investigation. Twenty years earlier, in a similar case in South Africa, he conducted a similar examination of a 365-foot rock-face.

After his close examination of the rock-face and the ground at the top, it was Dr Nagle's view that the dead girl could not have slipped, rolled or slithered down the crag. On the night of Helga's death, the grass at the top of the cliff was dry, Helga's shoes had a fairly good sole on them and, what's more, the edge of the cliff actually sloped upwards at the top before dropping sharply down to Radical Road.

Having studied the body, which suffered a fractured skull as well as a broken spine and fractures of both ankles, the doctor said he believed that the body had fallen from the top in a 'kind of swallow dive'. She had then struck and bounced away from rocks which projected out from the face about 28 feet down, before crashing head first on to the grassy path below. Had she merely slipped and fell, he said, he would have expected more superficial cuts and injuries, as she scrambled desperately to prevent herself from falling. No; he felt that either the dead woman had taken a running jump at the edge, or had been pushed – although he did concede that it was possible for someone to have been pushed along the edge of the cliff – not over it – and then to have stumbled and fallen.

The evidence took a somewhat strange turn when a prison officer was called to testify that he had taken the flyleaf of a book from a prisoner in Saughton Jail on which someone had handwritten a statement and drawn a schematic of the area of Salisbury Crags. The statement concerned a 'witness' who was supposedly sitting behind the couple on the cliff top that night, and described how Helga allegedly met her death.

The statement, made in the third person, said that there were 'two young peoples' on the hill at just after eight o'clock. The man was wearing 'dark trousers and a light coat'. The girl also had dark trousers but wore a dark coat.

The statement continued in its somewhat fractured English:

The moon did shine a little bit. He [the witness] sat down behind the young couple. They kissed together for much time, and did spoke. But the witness don't understood what was talking.

After about 15 minutes they kissed together, and shortly after they kiss they stood up. He did stood up slowly – she speedily. With one step she was behind him, and pushed him with both hands back. He only break down and did sat after this push on the stone ground. Then he stood up. She assault him with both hands, when he stood. He was staying near the slope. He seize her by the wrists, and she was trying to push him over the cliff. He took she to near of the slope. Then he pushed her away. She stumbled but she fell not down. She was now staying six to eight feet in front of him. Then he went away.

After five or six steps he heard a cry from her. He looked round and saw his wife fall down. He run to the cliff and cried her name 'Helga'. Then he run away to run for help.

The statement said that this 'witness' saw Helga standing at the edge and then become 'giddy' before she lost her equilibrium and fell down the slope.

The prisoner from whom this was confiscated said that it had been handed to him by Ernst Dumoulin who said 'That's what happened', and that God was his witness.

So now we had a slight change in the story. For some reason, Helga had decided to try and kill Ernst Dumoulin; he had defended himself and his wife had stumbled over the edge during the struggle. And the entire event had been witnessed by a nameless but apparently supernatural third party.

But why would Helga want to murder her new husband? She was, it would seem, hopelessly in love with him – certainly infatuated enough with him to run away from the security of her home in Germany to begin a new life in a foreign country. What had transformed her from a naïve young girl to an alleged mad murderess?

According to Dumoulin, the answer to that lay in the plot they had hatched together to make themselves a fortune.

They had been sitting in the boarding-house on their second night in Edinburgh discussing their future together, when he had mentioned, apparently as a joke, that they could defraud an insurance company. Helga was sitting on the bed and when he suggested this, she looked up at him and said, seriously, 'That's not a bad idea.'

They discussed the idea, formulating, revising and honing a plan that even Dumoulin admitted was far from perfect. It was an idea that is well known from countless films and television shows. Basically, he was to fake his own death and she would collect the insurance money.

Shortly after arriving in Edinburgh, he and Helga had indulged in a bit of sight-seeing and had visited the picturesque village of Cramond on the Firth of Forth. At low tide, they had walked along the causeway to Cramond Island and found a ruined building. Whilst making their plans, they recalled this site and decided to work it into their scenario. They had found a section where a portion of wall was missing, leaving a sheer drop to large boulders and the cold waters of the Forth. Ernst was to cut himself, leaving some spots of blood on the bricks alongside some personal belongings and on the rocks below. He would then make his way back to the mainland and disappear. Helga would then report his disappearance, wait a decent length of time before collecting the cash from the insurance company and meet up with Ernst again somewhere.

So, with this jointly formulated plan in mind, Dumoulin first approached the Bank of Nova Scotia and finally Hambro. Policies were taken out on both their lives to allay suspicion. The original plan was to use some of the cash loaned by the bank to pay the full premiums, but when that was not possible, they had to dip into their limited capital to pay only half. In doing so, Dumoulin thought that only one of the policies would be active, the one on his own life. It had not occurred to him that the policies may not have been processed.

On the afternoon following their wedding they made their first visit to Holyrood Park, walking along Radical Road, before returning to the Woods' lodging-house. They returned later that evening and, according to Dumoulin, sat down near the edge of Salisbury Crags, taking in the view. After they talked there for about an hour, they got up to leave. She came to him then gave him a kiss, which he thought was unusual because it was the first time she had made the initial move. He turned to go. And then, he claimed, she turned on him, pushing him hard between the shoulder blades towards the cliff edge.

'I turned my head towards Helga,' he told the court. 'She was standing behind me and I looked at her and she looked at me. Helga came towards me and I took her wrists. She was trying to push me towards the edge. The only chance I had was to get myself into a better position. I half turned and pushed her away. She stumbled. She turned round and she went over . . .'

He said he thought his wife was insane at that point and that he was sure 'God saved my life at that moment'. As he said that, Herr Konrad stood up in the public gallery and began to make his way forward towards the bench. However, court officers managed to block his path and he angrily left the courtroom. Dumoulin then proceeded to provide a visual display of what happened, with the court macer acting the part of Helga.

Later, Herr Konrad and his wife flew back to their home in Germany. They were not in court the following Monday to hear the jury find Dumoulin guilty of murder by an 11-to-four majority. They had been discussing their verdict for just over two hours. When she heard their guilty verdict, Dumoulin's mother (who was in court) cried out, 'Es ist nicht wahr!' – It is not true. She had to be helped from court. Once this had been done, the judge, Lord Wheatley, said to the court, 'I think we can appreciate the feelings of this unfortunate mother but we might also spare a thought for the unfortunate girl and her parents.'

Afterwards, when Lord Wheatley had sentenced Dumoulin to life for the murder of his wife in order to defraud the insurance company, the young Dutch National met with his parents before being taken back to Saughton. His mother, in tears, threw herself into his arms and he told her, 'You must be brave.'

In the end Dumoulin spent 15 years in Edinburgh's Saughton Prison, being released in 1987. During his time in prison, Dumoulin not only perfected his English and learned to play the trumpet, but also found religion after a German pastor presented him with a translation of the Bible. He began to study Divinity at Edinburgh University, being allowed out of prison every day to attend classes before returning to the prison at night. He did not try to hide his crimes from any fellow student with whom he struck a friendship, shamefully explaining that he was doing time for the murder of his wife and had to return to prison, whenever he was invited out for a drink at night. Because he was a serving prisoner he could not graduate at the end of the course, but the university did arrange for him to receive a non-graduate licentiate in Theology.

After his release, Dumoulin was deported to Germany, where he still lives. He is married now and has a family. He is a lay preacher and he uses his trumpeting skills in the church band. He also spends much of his spare time helping the handicapped.

His new wife knows all about his past and also knows that he has changed. In 1993, Dumoulin was found by a *Daily Record* reporter, who interviewed him about the events of 20 years before. Dumoulin admitted publicly for the first time that he had plotted to kill Helga, saying that he had been trying to wreak revenge on his father – who had apparently been responsible for the break-up of his first engagement – and God.

He said in the interview, 'At the time I was a very unhappy person with many personal problems in my life. I blamed God. I blamed my father. The only person I never blamed was myself.'

He was, he said simply, evil, and the thought of financial gain had never entered his head when he killed poor Helga, whom he admitted he had never loved.

Shortly after the trial in 1973, Herr and Frau Konrad arrived back in Edinburgh and commissioned the placing of a park bench on the Radical Road just below the spot on Salisbury Crags where their daughter was thrown to her death by an angry young man who wanted revenge on the world for his problems. Then they returned again to their farm near that tiny German hamlet, where Herr Konrad died shortly after. The bench is long gone now, but the Crags remain, rising sharply from the pathway and looking out over their city like a wall of stonefaced guardians, stoically standing their ground as they are buffeted by the wind and gouged by the rain.

Twenty years after those tragic events, another German family would be ripped apart by a violent act which took place in Scotland. But this time, the culprit would be a Scot. But the question which hangs over the terrifying and bloody affair is, why did it happen?

MURDER IN A CIVILISED COUNTRY

Architect Thomas Boedeker had thought long and hard about where to take his family for their annual vacation that year. They wanted to go touring in their camper, but so many European countries were too dangerous nowadays; there were too many stories of murderers and terrorists stalking the countryside on the continent. What he was looking for was a nice little country, with some beautiful scenery and plenty of things to do and see. Finally, he decided that the place for them was Scotland. It's a quiet place, he told friends and relatives, we will be safe there.

Unfortunately, he was proved wrong.

Certainly, much of Scotland – away from the cities – is quiet and safe and incredibly beautiful. There is plenty to do and see in this small country and tourists are (generally) welcomed warmly. For 364 days out of the year a visitor can come here, see the country, enjoy the scenery, take in the history and then return home with some tartan trinkets and some terrific photographs. But Mr Boedeker had the misfortune to arrive on the 365th day. He was, frankly, in the wrong place at the wrong time and he met up with a man carrying a gun.

In early July, Mr Boedeker, his wife, Renate (47), daughter, Julia (20), and son, Just (15), set out from their Stuttgart home, arriving in Britain on 6 July and spending their first night in the Lake District – the splendid views there acting as a taster for the rugged pleasures ahead – before heading north. On 7 July, 53-year-old Mr Boedeker parked his Volkswagen camper van on the shores of Loch Ryan, a sea loch cutting saltily into the Galloway coast towards the town of Stranraer – the main Scottish ferry port to Northern Ireland – and helping, along with the Irish Sea and Luce Bay to the south, to form the Rhins peninsula. But even closer to the makeshift campsite chosen by the family was Cairnryan, another ferry port. Later, this location would be cited by unnamed police sources as evidence of a possible and highly dramatic motive for murder.

Just before 10 a.m. on Thursday, 8 July, the Boedekers were having breakfast when a man of medium build but with a marked beer belly approached their caravanette. They saw he was carrying a revolver and a large knife. Concerned, Mr Boedeker left the van to meet him and his family heard the man shout, 'Money! money!' as they began to follow. But before Mr Boedeker could even reach into his pocket for his wallet, the man fired the gun twice. One bullet caught the tourist in the arm but the other sliced through his aorta, cutting off the blood supply both to and from the heart. He would have died within seconds.

Julia Boedeker ran forward and grabbed her father's wallet, handing it over to the man, but he shot her, too. Two bullets again, hitting her on the right leg and thigh, cutting into the femoral artery, sending the blood pumping out in a flood. Then he shot her mother, only once this time but it brought her down, the bullet nestling in her abdomen. Only 15-year-old Just managed to get away from the bloodbath, but not without injury. The gunman loosened off a shot at the boy's back as he sprinted away but, luckily, the bullet only caught him on the arm. The wound was bad enough and bleeding profusely, but Just, the adrenalin no doubt pulsing through his body, kept on running, not stopping until he reached the A77, the main road north from Stranraer to Glasgow.

Stranraer lorry driver James Allison (37) was driving north in his car, taking his wife, Mary (40), and 11-year-old daughter, Lisa, to Glasgow on a shopping trip when he saw the young man running along the centre of the road towards him, his arms flailing wildly, shouting at him to stop. Mrs Allison thought at first that the teenager was some sort of crazy person and told her husband not to stop, but Mr Allison slowed down anyway, fearing that there had been an accident somewhere and that someone was lying hurt. Panting and by now hysterical, the boy screamed, 'My father has been shot! My father is dead!' Mr Allison saw that the boy was bleeding from his arm and he kept asking for the police, saying repeatedly that his father was shot, that his mother and sister were still there, and that there was a madman with a gun and a knife. 'Please help! Please get the police, please . . .'

Mr Allison told the youth to get in the car and he sped to the Rhins of Galloway Hotel. When they pulled up outside the hotel Just shot out of the car and darted inside, again screaming about his family and calling for the police. A staff member gave him some brandy to calm him down while the police were alerted.

Three hours after the seemingly motiveless attack, police reached the murder scene. Armed officers had to be drafted in and precautions taken to ensure that the gunman was not still lurking in the area, waiting to pick off anyone else. When they got there they found Mr Boedeker dead and his wife and daughter in critical condition, not just from the bullet wounds but also hypothermia – they had lost a great deal of blood and the weather conditions that day were those of a typical Scottish summer, wet and blustery. In addition, the attacker had stabbed the two women, no doubt in an attempt to finish them off, before ransacking the camper. Julia had been stabbed in the back, one of the lunges puncturing a lung. Her mother had also been stabbed several times, some with such force that ribs had been broken. Later, X-rays would reveal several fragments of smashed bone in her lungs.

While the women were rushed to Garrick Hospital in Stranraer where they received emergency treatment – and then on to Dumfries and Galloway Royal Infirmary (Julia by helicopter, her mother by ambulance) – armed police set up roadblocks, stopping all traffic in and out of the area up to a distance of 29 miles. Tracker dogs sniffed across the rainswept countryside, while an RAF helicopter armed with heat-seeking equipment buzzed the leaden skies looking for signs of the escaping killer. They issued a description of the killer gleaned from the wounded German boy – between 40 and 50, about five foot, six inches tall, grey hair, pot-belly, wearing light jacket and trousers, possibly speaking with an English accent. However, residents of the immediate area were urged not to approach him if seen and, if possible, to remain in their houses with their doors locked.

It was the biggest manhunt this stretch of rolling countryside and rocky coastline has ever seen, with over 80 officers involved in casting the dragnet. But throughout that first day, the police had no sign of the killer, although a local woman did tell them of two sightings 24 hours before the shootings of an apparently crazed man. He fitted the general description of the man they were looking for, although he had an Irish accent. She had seen him twice, talking to himself and waving his arms around. She had even spoken to him, and he had told her he was from Londonderry.

That night, additional officers from Strathclyde Police joined their colleagues from the Dumfries and Galloway force to assist in the search. Then, about ten hours after the shootings, a farmer contacted the police to say he had spotted a man acting suspiciously on the A77 near his farm, walking towards Stranraer. Police converged on the spot and found 53-year-old Glasgow man James Boyce. Although he was unarmed he fitted the description issued, apart from the accent, and was taken in for questioning. He denied any involvement in the shooting, although detectives found four soggy Bank of England five-pound notes on his person. Boyce was one of the first people to be caught in the net and, at this stage, he was, in the words of police press releases, merely assisting them with their inquiries. But later, when Julia regained consciousness and was able to tell waiting officers what had happened, they learned she had handed the man cash before he shot her. It was then that the full significance of the bank-notes was realised. The serial numbers matched a batch of new Bank of England notes received by Mr Boedeker's German bank. And when Just attended an identification parade and picked Boyce out with no hesitation, the man's fate was sealed. When he appeared at Stranraer's Sheriff Court to be charged on Monday, 12 July, hundreds of people lined the streets to jeer and boo at him as he was led to and from the police van.

Boyce, from Rutherglen, was a married man with four children. He worked as a cleaner with Strathclyde Buses at a depot in Parkhead, and also carried out odd-jobs at a riding-stable just outside the city. A member of the Apprentice Boys of Derry, Boyce was a staunch Orangeman, allegedly deeply involved in raising funds for loyalist causes and who regularly attended the Walks in Belfast, catching the ferry at Cairnryan. But the Walk was not to take place until the weekend of 17/18 July. So why was he in the area over one week ahead of time? There are two different opinions about that.

He had a criminal record, although never for anything as serious as the crime for which he was now charged. His past offences were mostly for dishonesty – even a five-year conviction for assault and robbery received in 1987 did not involve the use of a firearm. His defence would later insist that he was in the south of Scotland simply to carry out a robbery and that he chose the Boedekers as victims. That was one possible explanation for his presence in the area at that time.

The gun and knife were never found despite an extensive search but there is a host of places in the area – remote lochs, dense woodland, not to mention the rocky coastline – where such weapons could be disposed of and never seen again. The bullets taken from the victims were analysed by ballistics experts and deemed to have been fired from a .45 Second World War revolver. Meanwhile, a search of Boyce's locker at his place of work revealed a supply of 9mm shells for use in a quite different weapon.

Both mother and daughter survived the attack, although for a while it was touch and go for Mrs Boedeker. Julia was transferred to Glasgow's Western Infirmary for treatment but Renate had to remain in Dumfries's Intensive Care Unit, as she was too sick to be moved. Doctors had said she had a ten to 15 per cent chance of life. But, after careful treatment and massive and repeated blood transfusions, she and her daughter were eventually allowed home.

They were not in the High Court of Glasgow in October 1993 to hear James Boyce admit his crimes. Throughout his police interviews he had denied any involvement, prompting one detective to call him 'cold, co-operative, uncomplaining and unthinking'. But one week before his trial was due to begin, he confessed to his counsel, Donald Findlay QC, who promptly lodged a Guilty plea. He was given two life sentences for the murder and attempted murders; the sentences to run concurrently. The judge recommended he serve a minimum of 20 years. As the judgment was pronounced, a loud sob burst from deep within the chest of a woman sitting in court and she ran out in tears. The Boedeker family were later informed of the verdict and resulting sentence at their home in Stuttgart. Meanwhile, a representative of the German Consul in Edinburgh, who had kept a close eye on the case from the very beginning, said that justice had been done.

But then came the second possible explanation for Boyce's presence at Cairnryan that day – and the reason why he killed Mr Boedeker and attempted to kill his family. The day Boyce began his double sentence, a daily newspaper printed unattributed quotes from police officers claiming that Boyce was no mere robber turned killer but was, in fact, a hit-man for the UDA. The unnamed officers were reported to have said that they believed Mr Boedeker had inadvertently uncovered a gang of loyalist weapons-smugglers operating in the Cairnryan area, and they had sent Boyce to silence him and make the 'hit' look like a robbery. The police said that the night he arrived in the area, Mr Boedeker set out from his camper to take photographs and he may have come upon the gang and even taken pictures. Not one of his three cameras, like the murder weapons, were ever found. The officers said that if robbery was the real motive, as the defence had claimed, why did Boyce not target a post office or a petrol station, or even a bank or a shop? Why pick on a family having breakfast in a quiet part of the countryside? And why kill the man before he even handed cash over? To support their theory, they pointed out that Boyce had strong loyalist sympathies; they claimed that the assault and robbery of which he had been convicted was to raise funds for terrorists; and revealed that a close relative of his had been sentenced to three years for trying to smuggle weapons to Ulster.

Certainly, the anonymous officers admitted that there was no evidence to support their claims, but pointed out that there was nothing to disprove them either. However, if Boyce was a UDA hit-man, is it likely he would use an old six-shot revolver to do the job? If he was part of a gun-running gang, then surely he would have had access to more efficient, more deadly weapons. And if his intention was to kill them all along, why ask for money in the first place? Certainly, he did not give his victim the chance to hand the cash over, and shot his daughter even after she had given him her father's wallet – but why not simply shoot them all right away and then make it look like a robbery? And surely a cold-blooded killer for the UDA would not have hung around the area for hours afterwards to be caught with incriminating bank-notes on his person.

Boyce himself merely told his counsel he was down there to carry out a robbery. And unless he changes that story, the police version of events will remain pure speculation.

Wasted Lives

VENDETTA

THE TINY VILLAGE of Dunure clings to the Ayrshire coast between the bustling town of Ayr to the north and the majestic splendour of the Robert Adam-designed Culzean Castle to the south. It is a picturesque little place – not much more than a shoal of attractive fishermen's cottages, a hotel, pub and restaurant and a harbour dotted with yachts and pleasure craft. And presiding over it all are the ruins of a castle which, like all self-respecting Scottish castles ruined or otherwise, has a dark and bloody history. For it was within these cold stone walls that Gilbert Kennedy, fourth Earl of Cassilis, ordered that Allan Stewart, the abbot of nearby Crossraguel Abbey, be stripped naked and roasted over an open fire until he agreed to surrender abbey lands to him. The abbot initially agreed but when he later reneged, the earl had him roasted again, this time basting him with hot oil for good measure.

Nowadays, life in Dunure is somewhat more peaceful. In the summer, motorists drive down the steep hillside from the roadway to enjoy lunch in the restaurant. Afterwards they may take a stroll around the harbour or along the shoreline and past the dark, forbidding castle tower, perhaps listening for the agonising screams of the tortured abbot which, they say, can still be heard on occasion echoing from the dark dungeon deep within its bowels. But in the summer of 1985, this small tourist trap became a different kind of trap for a man who had just blasted three workmates to death with a shotgun.

143

Peter McMurray had been working as a labourer at Bothwell Bank Sewage-Works, lying between Blantyre and Hamilton in Lanarkshire, for eight years. He had been glad to get the job, having been unemployed for a few months, and he vowed that he would keep it until he retired. One round of unemployment was enough for him and he wanted to support and provide for his family. But things did not go as planned. Within a month of his taking up employment, another man joined the workforce and the vendetta began.

Alex Sexton seemed to take an immediate dislike to the bearded, 43-year-old labourer. Soon, the two men were in open conflict and over the following eight years the tension built until it reached dangerous levels. What could be called childish pranks were played, although the hatred which smouldered at the heart of these 'pranks' made them something infinitely more sinister. McMurray was caught trying to slash Sexton's car tyres. Then McMurray found a white feather shoved into his locker. Both men's lockers were moved around and damaged. Excrement was smeared over padlocks and handles which either man was likely to touch, or poured into McMurray's boots. Masonic symbols were scrawled over a car brochure belonging to Sexton. It would appear there were faults on both sides. But no one, probably not even the killer, would have wanted it to end the way it did.

Sexton, it would seem, had a highly charismatic personality and was able to sway the opinions of some fellow workers against McMurray. They joined in the fun and games, eventually, in January 1985, banding together to send the man to Coventry, refusing to speak to him or work with him; treating him 'like a scab'. According to one fellow worker, McMurray said at this time that he would 'clear this place out before he was finished', and that 'they will know all about it, shortly'.

These stupid, senseless acts apparently took their toll on McMurray's physical and mental health. His personality changed from a happy, family man to a morose, silent individual who snapped and roared at his four children almost constantly. Normally a gregarious sort who loved family occasions, he began to shun his relatives, refusing on one occasion to act as best man at his brother's wedding and then failing to turn up at all. He even failed to attend his own daughter's christening. Instead, he turned to solitary drinking, apparently downing six or seven cans and a quarter-bottle of whisky every day. He seldom slept and when he did he railed against Alex Sexton and some of the other men, tossing and turning, shouting and swearing, moaning and murmuring. Finally, he went to his doctor who gave him tranquillisers to help him sleep.

He had at one time been a devout Christian but between 1982 and 1985, when much of the personality changes took effect, he stopped attending church. His wife said he lost interest in everything, including his personal hygiene and appearance. His work suffered, too. He would eat alone and took to disappearing for as long as two hours at a time.

He began to keep a secret journal, writing down what was happening to him at work, all the jolly japes, all the slights, all the snubs. He wrote about how they would empty teapots or kettles as he arrived for his tea and of how doors would be slammed in his face as he approached. At the back of it all, he wrote, was Alex Sexton who, he said, was 'the real scab. He's shopped all the staff, past and present.' He also wrote, 'Eight and a half years is too long to be under pressure. Something will have to be done.'

And early in 1985, he took £120 out of his savings and bought himself a shotgun.

At first his wife was extremely concerned at the purchase but he told her he wanted to use it to shoot ducks and rabbits at the nature trail near his work. She accepted what might be a new hobby for her husband, a new interest which should get him out of the house – and maybe out of himself. But the man started to show up at work with the shotgun in its case and the other workers began to grow worried about his demeanour. According to the wife of one of the co-workers, her husband was so concerned that he would phone home regularly during his shift to assure her he was all right.

Then, in July 1985, Alex Sexton was promoted to charge-hand. This would make him McMurray's immediate boss. According to another worker who asked McMurray what he thought of his, the man replied, 'I'm not bothered. I'm going to shoot the bastard anyway.' Shortly after news of the promotion, McMurray broke his hand and could not work. It was then, according to the prosecution, he set his murderous plans in motion.

Divorced 42-year-old Alex Sexton was on duty at the sewage-works on Wednesday, 24 July 1985, along with co-workers 56-year-old William McIntosh, who was married with one son, and 39-year-old father-of-two William Burns. There should have been a fourth man that day but, luckily for him, he was on holiday. At 8.30 a.m. the three workers were laughing and joking with the driver of a slurry tanker as he pulled out of the plant. Just over an hour later he drove back through the gates with another load and the sewage workers were nowhere to be seen, which was unusual. Then one of the lorry's crew noticed a thin trickle of smoke wafting up from a bothy used by the men as a canteen. They rushed over to the burning building and smashed a window to see inside. Through the thick, black smoke they could make out the bodies of the three men on the floor.

Someone phoned the emergency services, saying that it looked as if there had been some sort of explosion and fire, but when firemen forced their way through the smoke and flames they found the men had not been overcome by the fumes or caught by any explosion. When the bodies were turned over, they saw the wounds to their head and body. All three men had been shot to death at close range.

The police were then alerted but officers could not get into the bothy until the firemen were satisfied that there was no danger of any sort of gas explosion. Then, and only then, could the ground-work for the murder investigation begin.

It is likely that Peter McMurray's name was raised very early in the investigation although, as he could not be traced immediately after the discovery of the triple killing, he was not mentioned to the press. All reporters could say was that armed police were involved in a search for the killer, who may have escaped in the blue Datsun owned by Alex Sexton. Uniformed officers searched the area surrounding the sewage-works for the murder weapon but found nothing. This meant that the killer probably still had it, so although they were appealing for the public's help in finding the vehicle, they did urge people not to approach the man. He had already killed three men. He might not hesitate to kill again. The detective in charge of the case even went as far as to say that whoever did this was 'not right in the head'. While the nationwide alert was issued, armed police were standing by, waiting to move at a moment's notice should the man be spotted.

Meanwhile, relatives of one of the dead men, William Burns, arrived at the scene to identify the man's body. They had been informed that he was the victim of an accident but discovered on arrival that he had, in fact, been shot. Naturally, this news hit them hard.

In the meantime, Peter McMurray had driven in something of a daze to the Ayrshire coast, finally coming to a halt in the village of Dunure. He had no memory of killing the men. All he could recall was drinking three cans of beer, and washing down two painkillers with two mouthfuls of whisky before setting out for the nature trail beside the River Clyde, which runs alongside the works, to do some shooting. He remembered going into the bothy-cum-canteen in the plant to make a phone call. The men were all in there having their tea and McMurray later claimed that Sexton and one of the other men began to goad him as usual. Sexton said that he should have broken his neck and not his hand, adding, 'We are going to get rid of you for good anyway.' After that, he insisted, there was nothing. There was a slight memory of something burning his hand, like scalding tea, and the next thing he remembered was being in the car and on the road to Ayrshire. He kept seeing an image of the three men in his mind but was not sure if it was a memory or just a fantasy. He could not remember setting the building on fire to cover his tracks and the first he heard of the killings was on the car radio, which was when he realised what he must have done.

Once at Dunure, he wanted to kill himself. He had a five-gallon can filled with petrol in the car and the plan was to set fire to it. He went into the hotel bar and left a book with Sexton's name on it beside the telephone. He also told the owner's son to contact the police. Then, armed with a carry-out, he went back out and moved the car away from the buildings on the main street and settled down to pluck up the courage to take his own life. But as he sat there in the swiftly falling darkness, drinking his carry-out as the sound of the waves lapping against the harbour wall splashed in his ears and seagulls ducked and dived overhead, he fell asleep.

While McMurray slept, the publican's son dialled 999, telling the operator that the man they were looking for was in the village. Squads of armed police dashed to the coast. They moved quickly and silently as they surrounded the Datsun, their weapons trained on the doors. And then they waited for orders. Then, at about 2.00 a.m., they saw the interior light flicker on.

McMurray had woken with a start. He had been asleep for about four hours and had no idea what was happening. He clicked on the interior light and then opened the door and climbed out. As he stood up he found himself caught in the beams of high-powered lights set up by police and a voice was shouting at him not to touch the car. All he could see beyond the pool of bright light were shadows flitting back and forth. He raised his arms as instructed, shouting, 'Don't worry – I've done all the shooting I'm ever going to do. There will be no police widows tonight.' Then he lay down on the ground, his hands on the back of his head, while the marksmen moved slowly forward, their weapons still trained on him. One officer moved to the car and took the shotgun from inside, ejecting two live cartridges from the barrels. They also found the petrol can, pieces of paper and matches.

Later, when charged with the murders, police said McMurray nodded and commented, 'Sexton was giving me hassle for years. I felt like a different person when I'd shot them.'

At his trial in the High Court of Airdrie in November, McMurray admitted killing the three men but denied that he had plotted the murders, lodging a special defence of temporary insanity. He insisted he had no memory of the shooting itself. But the prosecution alleged he had planned the whole thing, that he had set out that morning with the express intention of killing Sexton and possibly some others, that he had calmly walked into the bothy and had begun blasting away, first at Sexton and Burns, who were blown to the floor, and then turning the second barrel on McIntosh.

And then came the act that would effectively destroy his allegation that he had not meant to kill. He stood over the wounded men and reloaded a further three times, eventually triggering a total of eight cartridges. Alex Sexton was found with wounds on his head and body; William Burns was wounded on the head and neck; William McIntosh on the neck, arm, armpit and knee. McMurray was standing so close as he did this that pellets gouged holes two inches deep into the cement floor beneath the bodies. McMurray then doused the bothy with petrol and set it alight in order to destroy any clues he may have left. The prosecution said that this showed a high degree of deliberation. This was no act of temporary insanity, it was argued, this was cold-blooded murder; an execution carried out by a person who had been feuding with Alex Sexton for years and who felt that the man's promotion above him was 'the last straw'.

The detective in charge of the investigation may have believed that the man responsible was 'not right in the head', but that was not the view of the psychiatrists who examined McMurray for the court. They not only declared him sane and fit to plead but also stated that they did not believe he was in any way deranged at the time of the murders – although it was pointed out that he had tried to kill himself twice, once by slashing his wrists in jail. However, reloading the weapon three times showed the killings were not impulsive, they said, and in their opinion he was responsible for his actions at the time. He did not appear to suffer from any depressive delusions, thought disorders or hallucinations. The fact that he seemed unable to recall anything about the murderous events was entirely possible; the shooting was probably too horrific for his mind to cope with and so had simply blanked it out. However, a psychiatrist appearing for the defence did say there was clear evidence of a depressive mental disorder. The court had already heard the accused's wife tearfully describe how her husband had turned from a kind and gentle and loving father into a silent, disturbed and bad-tempered stranger. She said that time and time again she begged him to leave the job but he refused. He had been unemployed for nine months and he had no wish to repeat that experience.

McMurray's defence hoped for a verdict of culpable homicide but in the end the jury found the man guilty of murder by an eight to six majority (one member had taken ill two days before the end of the trial). Peter McMurray was sentenced to a minimum of 20 years in prison, plus another three for setting fire to the bothy and stealing Sexton's car. As he was sentenced a voice rang out from the public benches saying, 'You should hang.' His wife burst into tears when she heard the news, repeating her disbelief that her husband was mentally ill and needed treatment not punishment.

Slowly, working life returned to normal at the Bothwell Bank Sewage-Works. New members of staff were drafted in to replace the dead men and their killer. The events of that blood-soaked day in July 1985 faded to a memory. Then, eight years later, they resurfaced when the plant was the site of another horrific find . . .

LOVE AND MONEY

The karaoke-machine was thumping out music at full volume when the three men walked into the bar. It was not what you might call a top-class establishment. In fact, it had been described as 'a bit of a howff' (a howff being old Scots for a shelter or meeting place, but more recently it is used to describe a place which is far from salubrious) so the men looked somewhat out of place in their smart crombie-style coats.

They looked around the busy bar-room, apparently seeing what they wanted on a small raised area towards the rear of the establishment. Two of them then moved to a fruit-machine near to this area.

The man they were looking for was George Hall and he was sitting at a table, apparently accompanied by a woman. He had come to this pub in Blantyre for a confrontation with the man who had been having an affair with his wife for some months, right under his own nose. He had known this man and had trusted him. He had conducted business with him. He had invited him into his *home*.

On the other hand, and it is perhaps doubtful that this even crossed his mind as he waited in the pub, his own attitude to his wife had not helped matters. According to the stories heard in court later, Hall was a violently jealous man who abused the woman both physically and mentally. He had also, allegedly, made threats not only against the man with whom she had fallen in love but the man's children and had – again allegedly – begun an affair with his wife in an effort to draw him out.

And so he sat in this down-market bar, listening to the people enjoying themselves, sipping a drink and watching the door, waiting for the man to come in.

He probably did not know what happened. He may have seen one of the men who had just entered aim something at him from under the material of his coat but if he did, he did not have time to move before the weapon was fired.

Witnesses said they heard two very quiet 'popping' sounds, one after the other, and the man slumped forward in his seat, hitting his head on the table as he went down. There was blood on his face, one said, but she had presumed he had injured himself as he struck the table. At the time she presumed he was drunk.

The revelry continued as the two men at the fruit-machine moved swiftly over, picked the man up from the floor and carried him through the bar, past the small dance floor and out the back way. No one knew what had happened. No one paid any attention. The woman who had been sitting at his side did not seem to be bothered in the slightest by what had happened. She had, apparently, shuffled in her seat a bit when the man fell, but did not go to help him. Whoever this woman was, she was never seen or heard from again but it is probable that she had nothing to do with the murder. The customers who had seen the man fall were assured that he just had had too much drink – a common enough occurrence after all – and would be looked after by his friends. No one was able to identify the woman or the three men.

Then someone appeared from the other side of the bar with a mop and a bucket and cleaned up the small pool of blood forming on the floor and tidied away the broken glass. Some months later, crusts of this blood could still be seen in the bucket and in other parts of the bar.

It would be three months before George Hall's body would be seen again.

Charge-hand Stephen Kane had clocked on for work in Bothwell Bank Sewage-Works at quarter to eight on 5 January 1993. His first task that day was to check the plant's screens, which catch any large pieces of debris that find their way into the effluent. He was not surprised to find them blocked. They were often blocked. But what did surprise him was that part of the blockage appeared to be caused by a human leg.

It was not yet fully light at that time on a January morning and at first Mr Kane thought someone had thrown a tailor's dummy into the works. However, one of his workmates went to his car and turned on his headlights to provide more light. It was no dummy. What they were looking at were human remains, complete with a shoe still attached to one of the legs and a piece of blue plastic rope around the torso.

151

Recovering a body from any site is grisly enough, but when it has been immersed for some time in sewage the revulsion factor is doubled. But there was one further macabre development to come, for when horrified police gingerly fished the body out of the sludge, they found that the lower part of the arms had been hacked off.

The discovery sparked off a full-scale hunt, first to identify the remains found in the sewer and then to find his killer, or killers. Their investigations uncovered a harrowing tale of love and hate; of violence, drugs and alleged gun-running; of a marriage which had descended into a nightmare of abuse and jealousy.

What it failed to unearth was the identity of the person who pulled the trigger.

The body was of a stockily built male, about five foot, eight inches tall. When examined by Doctor Marie Cassidy, consultant forensic pathologist at Glasgow University, she could see that, as well as the obvious mutilation of the arms, there were other substantial injuries – 35 in total – including multiple fractures of the skull, upper arms and legs. The body had also been burned, no doubt in a bid to make any identification impossible. The pathologist said parts of it were 'like a roast in the oven'; the heat being so intense it may have caused the bones to crack. It was lying in a 'pugilistic position'. Also known as 'heat-stiffening', the effect causes the arms and legs to ape a boxer's stance in the ring: hands up by the face, legs slightly crouched. Intense heat causes the muscles to weld on to the limbs' flexor surfaces and then contract.

The face had three scars on the face and neck; one underneath the chin, another on the mouth and the third on the left-hand side of the neck. The body was, according to the doctor, quite literally coming apart as she examined it and because of this she was unable to say which injuries had been inflicted post mortem and which before death. She could not even say if the loss of the forearms was the result of a deliberate act of dismemberment by the killer or if it was caused naturally as it moved within the sewage-works.

What she was certain of, however, was that the man had been murdered.

A second search of the sewage-works by police had unearthed pieces of the skull, which was so badly fractured that Dr Cassidy had to piece it together like a jigsaw puzzle. Once she had done this, she found there were pieces missing which should have been there, and something present that should not have been naturally. The pieces which were missing were fragments of skull and the dead man's brain. The foreign item was a spent and malformed .22 bullet.

The bullet was found in the gap between the bottom of the skull and the top of the spine. She then tried to ascertain where the point of entry had been, concluding that it was just behind the right ear. Judging by the angle of the entry hole and evidence of powder burns, the firearm had been fired down towards the victim at close range at an angle of between 45 or 20 degrees. Without access to the gun which fired the shot, she could not say for certain just how close the killer had been standing to the man when he pulled the trigger, but she estimated that he was no more than four feet away.

Death had occurred very quickly afterwards because there was no evidence of bleeding. Either that, or this particular injury was caused after he was already dead, perhaps as a *coup de grâce*. While Dr Cassidy was conducting her thorough post mortem, the police were trying to find out who the dead man was. By the end of the month they were fairly certain that it was George Hall, who had been reported missing on 29 October 1992 by his brothers. He had not been seen since 9 October. Mr Hall had two very distinctive tattoos on his forearms and it was suspected that the reason the forearms were removed from the body was to prevent identification.

George Hall was married, for the second time, with one young daughter. When police had asked his wife, Jacqueline, about her husband just after he was reported as missing, she told them that on 9 October they had been going into Glasgow for a meal to celebrate her birthday. Her husband had gotten into an argument with a taxi-driver, she said, and when she intervened he told her to 'fuck off!' and then walked away. She never saw him again.

When asked why she had not reported him missing she told the officers, 'I don't care if I never see him again.' She got her wish.

By that time, early November 1992, Mrs Hall was living with another man. George Carlin was a self-employed financial adviser who had met the Halls the previous year when he negotiated a mortgage for them. On 11 November 1992 he was interviewed by the police about Hall's disappearance and he said the last time he had seen the man was six weeks before he vanished. No doubt police were suspicious, but with no evidence at that stage of any foul play, there was little they could do. Then, the following year, the body was found in the sewer.

By the end of January 1993, when they had reached their conclusion the body was that of George Hall, officers called at the Glasgow west-end premises of the School of Motoring owned by the Halls to again talk to Jacqueline Hall. After the interview she was crying and very distraught.

Soon, police arrested Mrs Hall and George Carlin. The lovers, as well as two other men, James Nicholas and Raymond Allison (not his real name), were charged with murdering George Hall by repeatedly shooting him in the head and body. They were said to have been acting with another or others in the act.

Allison and Nicholas were also accused of dismembering and burning the body and concealing it in the sewage system in a bid to destroy evidence and defeat the ends of justice. Allison was charged with setting fire to the car which was allegedly used in the commission of the crime and throwing the firearm used into the River Clyde at the Red Bridge near Blantyre Farm Road, Uddingston. He was also alleged to have attempted to induce witnesses to provide him with a false alibi and therefore attempt to pervert the course of justice. All four accused denied the charges.

The trial began in the High Court at Edinburgh on 10 August 1993. It was expected to run for a number of weeks but in the end lasted just over three, including a two-day delay in the final week when one juror was taken ill (by that time, the jury had already been reduced to 14 because of the illness of another juror at the beginning of the trial). From the start, both the Crown and Defence agreed that some photographs of the body should not be shown to the jury because they were too gruesome.

The defence hammered away at the claim that the murder victim was not only violently abusive towards his wife but was also a drug- and arms-dealer. The jury was told that police were apparently interested in the man regarding a cheque-book fraud and that he had a number of shady friends. They heard that George Hall was a black belt in karate and shortly before he was murdered had been declared bankrupt. However, they also heard that he had

£12,000 in cash hidden away in his home. Members of the deceased's family refuted all these suggestions, saying that if Jacqueline Hall had been abused, they had never seen any evidence of it.

Police found a witness who said that George Carlin had told him that Hall had argued with his wife while on a night out and had driven off. The witness had asked Carlin if he was worried that Hall would return and find him living with his wife, but Carlin allegedly replied that Hall would not be back because he had heard that the man had been shot in a pub in East Kilbride – a sprawling new town to the south-east of Glasgow – and his car blown up.

Carlin also alleged to this witness that his friend, Raymond Allison, had done it at his instigation.

But Hall had not been shot in East Kilbride. He had actually been lured to Blantyre, which lies between the town and Hamilton, in particular, to the Cobblers Bar; a pub, it was claimed in court, which Carlin and Raymond Allison had been thinking of buying. And there someone pumped a bullet into George Hall's brain.

Police said that another customer had told them that he had heard a crack and saw a drunk man being carried out of the bar. According to his statement, he had gone over to where the man had fallen and saw blood on the floor. A man called 'Nicky' (James Nicholas) had asked him to give him a hand to clean it up but he had refused, saying he did not want to be involved.

Police found the bucket and discovered the rusty traces of blood in it and on the mop. The body was in too advanced a state of decomposition to extract blood samples, so the controversial science of DNA fingerprinting was used to make the all-important identification link between the blood in the bucket and the dead man. To do this, they took samples from Hall's mother and father, as well as his first wife and their two children, because DNA can be traced back to an individual's parents. The samples were then compared with specimens of blood from the bucket. As far as the police and forensic experts were concerned, there was a match.

The following morning, the witness told police, he met Raymond Allison, whom he claimed had also been in the bar that night, and told him that what had happened in the Cobblers the previous night had been 'fucking out of order'. To this the accused man allegedly replied, 'No, it's all right, everything's all right.'

However, when it came for his time in the witness box, the witness claimed that he had made the tape-recorded statement under police pressure. He claimed they threatened to charge him with murder unless he made a statement implicating Raymond Allison. The same witness also claimed that George Carlin had previously offered him cash, saying he wanted 'something taken care of'. He said that Carlin mentioned two men he wanted 'sorted out'. The witness claimed that Carlin was offering other people money for the same thing and one or two accepted the cash, including himself. He received, he said, £5,000 from Carlin and promptly went on holiday with the money and later bought a car. He admitted in court that he had effectively conned Carlin out of the cash because he had no intention of sorting anyone out.

Another witness said that Carlin had paid him £500 to arrange a phoney drug deal with George Hall. The idea was that he would then run the man down with his car. In the end, the alleged meeting was only used as a diversionary tactic to allow Jacqueline Hall the chance to leave her husband.

On the thirteenth day, George Carlin dramatically changed his plea from Not Guilty to Guilty, admitting that he had murdered George Hall, along with others, although he had not been present in the pub when the gun was fired. James Nicholas also admitted being involved in the disposal of the body and had the murder charge against him dropped. Jacqueline Hall had her Not Guilty plea accepted by the Crown. She left the court and was whisked away in a car by friends.

That left only Raymond Allison in the dock. He still denied all the charges against him, claiming that two other men had actually cut up and dumped the body. One of the men he named was his own brother.

As soon as Carlin and Nicholas pled guilty, the trial was halted to give both the Crown and Allison's defence team time to obtain statements from them. It was thought Carlin, Nicholas and Jacqueline Hall would all give evidence in the trial but, ultimately, only one of them took the stand.

George Carlin told the court that he and Jacqueline had begun their affair in September 1991. Two months after that, Mrs Hall had left her husband for the first time to live with Carlin in Eastwood, a suburb on the city's southside. At that time, George Hall did not know that she was leaving him for another man, let alone his friend, George Carlin, who was still giving him financial advice during this period. Carlin said that Hall often told him he was trying to trace his runaway wife. In March the following year he did manage to track his wife down and she decided to return to him while Carlin found them somewhere else to stay. The suggestion was that if Hall had found out about the affair, there would have been violence.

Throughout the trial, the defence had suggested that Hall was a drug-dealer, claiming that he owed a substantial amount of money to the so-called 'Drummy Crew', a gang of drug-dealers based in Drumchapel, a housing estate on Glasgow's northside. Carlin also claimed that Hall was an arms-dealer who stashed his goods in Drumchapel's Bluebell Woods. He alleged that he had actually seen him with not only a shotgun, but also an Uzi sub-machine-gun and a kalashnikov rifle. He said that he had once come upon Hall cleaning the kalashnikov just as Hall found a bullet stuck in the weapon's chamber. The man was apparently trying to dislodge the bullet with a knitting needle. Carlin said he told Hall not to be daft, but Hall replied he was an expert. Certainly, Hall had been in the Marines for 14 months, but that, obviously, did not make him an expert.

Whether the Drummy Crew actually exists is a matter open to conjecture. There are, of course, drug-dealers in the area, but whether they call themselves by that name is not clear. As for the arms cache, no evidence has – as far as is known – been uncovered.

However, as was perhaps inevitable, the affair was ultimately discovered. In May 1992, Carlin and Jacqueline Hall went on holiday to Florida, with the Halls' baby daughter, during which George Hall unsurprisingly found out all about their liaison. According to Carlin, threats were made to shoot them on their return. The police took the claims seriously enough to organise an escort for them at Glasgow Airport. Hall, incensed by the police interfering in his personal life, lodged a complaint against officers involved. The complaint died with him.

Meanwhile, the lovers took flight; moving around Scotland, staying in hotels, lodging with friends and even spending nights in carparks. When they had run out of money, Jacqueline Hall again decided she would have to return to her husband. They were all exhausted and a life on the run was no way to bring up a one-year-old child.

Although George Hall did not know where Carlin lived, he did have the man's mobile phone number. According to Carlin's testimony, Hall would phone him up at all hours of the day and night, making threats. He once threatened to nail Carlin to a tree, pour petrol over him and set him alight in front of Carlin's own children. He said Hall also threatened to kill his children.

'I don't think you know what fear is until you are in that position,' he told the court.

Something would clearly have to be done and Carlin claimed that he had mentioned his problem to his friend, Raymond Allison, who offered first to break George Hall's legs. Carlin, however, said that he believed the only way to stop him was 'to take him off the planet'. A figure of £3,000 was agreed for the 'hit'.

Their first idea was to somehow lure George Hall to a lonely road where he would then be shot – a plan rejected because it was believed that the man would come mob-handed and no one wanted to be involved in a gunfight. Then it was decided that Carlin would entice him to the Blantyre Bar, which they had planned on buying. 'If I could get him out to the Cobblers Bar,' said Carlin in court, 'I was told he would not leave.'

George Hall did leave the bar, but perhaps not alive.

Carlin phoned the proposed victim and suggested a meeting in the pub. He waited across the road in his car, watching for Hall's arrival. When the man rode up in a taxi, Carlin said he phoned the pub on his mobile and said to whoever answered, 'That's him, there.' He had no idea who took his call but he said he had been assured that everyone in the bar knew what was going to happen. If that was the case, then it was a conspiracy doomed to failure. There is always someone who will talk to the police.

He waited ten minutes until he received a call saying, 'That's it done.'

Later that night, he claimed he spoke to Allison and asked him what had happened, hoping he would say he had shot Hall in the legs or something along those lines. The man allegedly replied, 'That's it.'

'What do you mean?' Carlin asked.

'That's him away. He won't bother you again.'

Next day, Allison allegedly said he had shot George Hall. A horrified Carlin asked, 'What, in a crowded pub?'

'Yes, it's okay. Everything is fine,' assured the other man.

But Carlin's fingering of Raymond Allison for the slaying was not enough. On the eighteenth day of the trial, the judge, Lord Caplan, ruled there was insufficient evidence to convict Allison following a submission from the accused's counsel that there was no case to answer. On making his ruling, Lord Caplan referred to Carlin's testimony that Allison had been paid to murder George Hall.

'I do not know what you made of that,' the judge told the jury, 'but that is not the point because under our law it would have to be corroborated. There would have to be other evidence to enable you to decide, if it was your inclination to do so, that Carlin was telling the truth about Mr (Allison).

'In my view there is no corroboration. There is quite insufficient evidence to corroborate what Carlin said. Whether he was telling the truth or not, and I do not know, the accused cannot be convicted on that evidence.'

Raymond Allison walked from the High Court a free man.

George Carlin was then sentenced to 25 years for the murder of George Hall and James Nicholas to five years for helping dispose of the corpse. Nicholas had admitted being in the Cobblers that night and to going to see what was happening in the kitchen where the man had been taken after the shooting. That was how he got some of the blood on him. There, a man he knew – not one of the accused it was emphasised – had asked his help in disposing of the body. He had agreed, whether out of fear of this man or misplaced loyalty it is not known, but insisted he did not physically take part in either the dismemberment or the burning. However, he had been there and had accepted his responsibility.

And so what was perhaps one of the most gruesome cases to be heard in a Scottish court for some years came to an end. But the identity of the man who pulled the trigger remains a mystery. James Nicholas's wife and his father said they knew who the killer was and that James was protecting the man by not naming him. The family of the dead man also gave two names to the police, although a few days after telling reporters this, Hall's sister and other relatives had pooled financial resources to offer a one-thousand-pound reward for information leading to the conviction of the guilty person.

Suspicions there may be, but no proof. No one has been arrested for the shooting. Meanwhile, the man Carlin tried to pin it on, Raymond Allison, was subsequently convicted of threatening a bar manager with a shotgun in an incident which took place about five days after George Hall's body had been found. Allison was charged with taking the manager into the office of the Airdrie pub, telling him that he was 'getting it' and then backing out of the pub with another man, waving the shotgun at customers.

But one such conviction does not a murderer make. Somewhere out there is a killer who has evaded justice. And he is not alone . . .

A Question of Justice

HARD CASES

A MURDER IS probably one of the most difficult cases to investigate. Although not always as contrived as its fictional counterpart, such an investigation can involve so many conflicting emotions, so many different motives, so many complex characters that sometimes it seems incredible that it is ever solved at all.

And even when a conviction has been gained and the appeal predictably refused and the culprit safely behind bars, there may yet be little corners of the case cloaked in shadows. For it is true that when all is said and done in some cases, things can still be said although very little can be done. In other words, when the murder investigation has run its course and a conviction has been gained and the appeal has been dismissed, there may still be questions for which there are no easy answers.

Such a case took place in the small town of Tullibody, lying between Alloa and Stirling. It was a particularly brutal killing, made even more terrifying by the seeming lack of motive. And because the young man ultimately convicted of the crime was found standing over the body soon after death and eventually confessed, it would appear to be open and shut.

However . . .

The blocks of tenement flats on Tullibody's Alloa Road were being renovated and their tenants decanted, among them 70-year-old former miner Samuel Murray, a well-known and well-liked man in the area. Luckily, he was not moving far from his home at number

69 Alloa Road, merely round the corner to number 1 Blackmuir Place, a bottom flat at the edge of a row of terraced houses.

At around 7.30 p.m. on 18 June 1992, Mr Murray arrived at the Top Club, a working-man's drinking-house in Tullibody. He stayed there for around three hours, downing four or five pints of beer, after which he took a taxi home. The taxi-driver chatted to him on the way, noting that the old man was not drunk and although he generally had a little trouble walking, Mr Murray was able to get into his house unaided. The taxi-driver then pulled away, completely unaware that he was to be the last person to see Mr Murray alive. Apart from whoever killed him.

A witness said Mr Murray's light was still burning at 11.30 p.m., but by one in the morning, when a night-watchman was making his rounds of the flats being renovated, the light was off.

Then, at about 2.45 a.m., an 80-year-old widow who lived in Muirside Road (a short distance from Mr Murray's flat) was awakened by the sound of her doorbell chiming. She looked at her clock as she got up, wondering who it could be at that time of night, and went to the front door, although she prudently did not open it. Shouting through the closed door, she queried the intruder's identity and heard a young man's voice asking, 'Could you take me in and put a plaster on?'

The elderly lady refused to let him in and went back to her bedroom. From the window she saw the young man walking away from her garden. She said he appeared to be trying to cover his face with his left arm as he walked away. She also said that he was outside her door for about 15 minutes.

Shortly after 3.00 a.m., the night-watchman was walking past Mr Murray's flat again and this time he noticed that the bedroom lights were back on. He knew the old man and it occurred to him that something might be wrong, so he moved to the front door and called out Mr Murray's name, peering through the frosted glass panel as he did so. Inside, he said later, he could hear a shuffling noise and saw a figure, crouching down in the hallway, as if on all fours. The door was lying ajar so he pushed it open and saw a young man backing off down the hall. He recognised him as Derek Johnstone, who lived locally. He also said he saw a small carpet knife, he thought blue in colour, lying in the hallway in front of a large box.

'Chris, help me!' said the young man, 'The old man's been stabbed.'

Samuel Murray lay on the bathroom floor. He had been stabbed – and more. Much, much more. The horrific wounds he had received were the result of not only a frenzied and quite brutal attack but also a calmer, more calculated bout of sadism. The poor man was apparently struck over the back of the head with a large piece of building-block, which was found in the toilet bowl, and his throat cut from the right-hand side three times, slicing one inch into the muscles and leaving a wide, gaping wound seven inches long. The voicebox was crushed with pieces of the smashed thyroid cartilage, which helps support the voicebox, obstructing the air passage. The cricoid cartilage, which also supports the voicebox, and the hyoid bone were also fractured. These injuries were caused, in the opinion of the pathologist, by heavy crushing blows to the front of the neck. This alone would have inevitably caused death, even if treated immediately.

The jaws and nose were broken. There was a patterned abrasion on the forehead comprising of four parallel lines where the killer had used a straight-edged weapon to batter the old man. The face and scalp had been ripped open by no less than 17 cuts, while the left eye had been punctured. There was another patterned bruise on the front of the chest. The prosecution tried to insist that this pattern was left by the accused's footwear but it may also have been caused by the same weapon which left the marks on the forehead. Twelve of the man's ribs were fractured. There were many other bruises and abrasions on the body and face.

But then came the sadistic element. Whoever had first hit the man with the brick, then cut his throat and slashed at his face before either hitting him several times on the head and body with either a weapon with a straight edge and/or stamped on him, was not yet finished. Whoever did it then coldly peeled back Mr Murray's shirt and vest and proceeded to carve 17 shallow cuts on his abdomen. Whoever did this enjoyed the sensation of slicing flesh. Whoever did this liked his work.

And if all that was not enough, there were two further stab wounds to the stomach, one of which, caused by a single-edge blade, could have proved lethal even if treated.

But at this stage, all the night-watchman could see were the wounds to the elderly man's head and face as well as some to the body. And the blood. There was a lot of blood, dripped and smeared on the floor, spread out like a bright-red halo on the wall around the head and spattered on the ceiling. Johnstone's hands, too, had some blood on them and by now he was beginning to panic, screaming, 'Help me! Help me! Get an ambulance.'

According to the night-watchman, Mr Murray was still alive at this point. He said he asked him who had done this to him and he saw the old man's eyes turn to Johnstone. This, however, was unlikely – the man was, without a doubt, already dead by this time so any eye movement detected may merely have been involuntary. The night-watchman then told Johnstone to stay where he was while he telephoned for an ambulance. Then he turned and left the house. Once outside he realised that the young man had followed him and he again told him to stay in the house. Then he sprinted off to his telephone.

While he was gone, Johnstone tried to attract more help, banging on doors and crying, 'Come quick! Come quick! There's a man bleeding to death down the road!' But no one else came, although one woman phoned the police, and Johnstone went back into the death house to do what he could for the man. During this period, the prosecution said, he also picked up the knife from the hall floor and threw it, as well as a length of bloody wood apparently used in the beating and a bottle of rum, into neighbouring gardens.

However, a witness who said he had heard cries of 'Help!' and someone saying 'come on' between 3.05 a.m. and 3.10 a.m., said he saw the night-watchman and Derek Johnstone talking on Mr Murray's steps at 3.17 a.m. He continued to watch after the old man left but, he said, he did not see Johnstone leave again. Someone else said he thought he heard people running through the close at just after 3 a.m.

The police arrived at 3.20 a.m. to find the night-watchman back at the house and Johnstone in the bathroom on his hands and knees, trying to apply first-aid to a dead man. They noticed that the front of the young man's T-shirt was ripped at the front. They looked around the flat and found that it was in considerable disarray. Someone had obviously searched both the bedroom and living-room, rifling through his possessions and throwing them on the floor.

Johnstone was removed from the immediate area and agreed to attend Alloa Police Station voluntarily, where, at about 4.00 a.m., a police-constable took a statement from him. And he told the first of his stories.

He said he had been in a pub until about 1.30 a.m. and had left with a friend to walk home. His friend left him soon afterwards and he walked on to Banchory Place where he met another friend outside a school. He had talked to him for about half an hour and then his friend left him to go to another pal's house. Johnstone then said that he walked past the garage, past a Pakistani grocer's shop and then turned left into Blackmuir Place.

'I heard a scream,' he told the officer, 'but I thought it was just a man and wife fighting, it was a rough scream but I knew it was coming from a man. I walked up a wee bit until I was level with the old man's living-room and I heard another scream. I heard it coming from the house. I went back and walked up the path and round to the guy's door.

'I chapped it once; there was no answer. I chapped again and walked into the lobby. I saw the blood on the toilet door. I turned round and saw the guy lying on the floor of the toilet.

'I went to the bedroom and picked up two cloths which were lying on the floor next to the dressing-table. I went back to the toilet and soaked the cloths with cold water and put the first cloth on his throat. There was a cut there, it was very deep and wide. I started [to] dab his face with the second cloth because he was covered in blood. I then checked his pulse on his right arm with my right hand but I couldn't feel any pulse.

'I then began to push his chest because I have been shown about survival and first-aid in the TA [Territorial Army]. He started speaking again. He shouted for help twice.

'I got up – I was kneeling by his left side – and ran to the front door where I met Chris (the night-watchman). I told him to stay with the old man while I would go and tell the old man's daughter, Catherine Murray. Chris told me to stay with him and he would go and phone for an ambulance. I went back to the old man and pushed his chest again but he wouldn't come back.'

But after that initial statement there was an addition in the police officer's notebook, as if Johnstone had just remembered it or was, perhaps, responding to a question.

'When I came up the path and walked round the house I saw two guys running next to the old man's garden. They were moving across a garden towards a close. They went through the close and I don't know where they went after that.'

Johnstone said that one of the people he saw was about five foot, ten inches tall, between 18 and 20 years of age, with blond hair. He was wearing a green sort of sweatshirt with white writing on the back, blue jeans and white trainers or shoes. The other was smaller, about five foot, four inches, with dark hair, and he was wearing a white T-shirt with sleeves just below his shoulders, blue jeans and dark trainers or shoes.

Johnstone signed the entry in the police officer's notebook. That was his initial statement. Within a few hours, he would apparently change that and tell a different, more incriminating story. And even later, he would change it again. He would also tell a number of different stories about the earlier part of the evening (however, for this account I have concentrated mainly on the period immediately before and after the murder). Certainly, this constantly changing story did not help his case at all. However, there may be reasons for that.

Derek Johnstone was then 18 years of age, of below average intelligence and had a history of drug abuse. He was not a mainliner – injecting directly into his veins – but he was an abuser all the same, admitting to snorting various substances in the past and habitually taking drugs in tablet form. During the day immediately before the murder he had taken a total of six Nitrazeram tablets, prescribed by his doctor to help him sleep, and six 'jellies' – capsules filled with the valium derivative Temazepam. When asked where he got these drugs, he said he bought them from a man at the chip shop, but police could not trace the alleged dealer.

Johnstone had also drunk several cans of beer and smoked a reefer. This, coupled with the other substances ingested by him, would have made him severely disorientated and, considering he had also been helping to dig a garden for several hours in the late afternoon and evening before going out drinking, extremely fatigued. When he was examined by a doctor in the police station at 9.15 a.m. the following morning, after being charged with the murder, he was 'rather red-eyed' and was 'undoubtedly fairly sleepy'. He was also 'rather giggly' and made comments which the doctor thought were 'obviously inappropriate in view of the seriousness of the allegation'. The comments displayed a belief that he would be home quite soon.

But by the time of that examination, Johnstone had already confessed to the crime. While still being treated as a witness, Johnstone was interviewed (the police said he declined to have this taped) and had been asked how his T-shirt came to be ripped. He said that it had been caused during a fight with 'a Paki'. He was also asked how his clothes came to be bloodstained and he said that he must have got it on him when he was trying to help the dead man.

He was then asked if he remembered seeing a knife on the floor beside Mr Murray. Johnstone said he did not. (The knife had somehow disappeared after being seen by the night-watchman and was subsequently found at 5.50 a.m. following a search of the gardens behind the house. However, it also has to be pointed out that the night-watchman said he had seen it on the hall floor, not directly beside the body.) The officers had then grown suspicious and the young man's status swiftly switched from witness to suspect and he was duly cautioned. Johnstone was said to have replied, 'I'd tain six jellies and drink as well, I was pished. I knocked the door and Sammy came. I goes, can I come in and he says aye. I just went into the toilet and I skelped him wi' a brick, I skelped him over the heid then I kicked him on the heid, that was it. Then I had the knife and I was goin' to cut him *but he was already cut.*' [my italics]

Johnstone signed this entry in a detective constable's notebook and he was then arrested. During the taped interview that commenced at 6.50 a.m., his earlier confession was repeated to him and he agreed he had said it. He also said he had thrown the knife away in a garden, to the right of the flat where it landed in the grass – which the police already knew. He said his T-shirt was torn because he had ripped eyeholes in it to cover his face as he stood at the wall of the house. He didn't want Sammy – whom he knew – to recognise him.

'But why did you not want him to recognise you?' he was asked. 'What were you gonnae do?'

'I wis gonna . . . to kill him, 'cos I . . .' Johnstone said, his stammer very apparent. ' . . . to hit him and run away but . . .'

'Uh-huh,' said the officer.

'When I hit him, he hit his head against the toilet.'

He did not know why he was going to the house, and said he

had no reason to hit the old man, saying, 'I'm the only guy that used to go doon and see him a' the time.'

He was adamant that he did not search the house. And during the interview he was obviously confused and unclear about exactly what had happened. He could give no details about the other injuries to Mr Murray and even amended his initial statement that he had put the makeshift mask on when he went to the door at first, saying instead that he put it on after he got in! He could not give any explanation as to why he would have done this after the old man had already seen him. He claimed the old man shouted for help twice – presumably this would have been before his voicebox was shattered – and Johnstone said he went to get help, too.

He said he got the knife from Mr Murray's kitchen but did not use it because, he repeated, the man was cut already. 'He probably cut it . . .' he began, '. . . cut himself when he fell against the toilet.'

So, Derek Johnstone was confessing to this quite horrendous crime. Later, the prosecution said that although he was obviously under the influence of drink or drugs, which were slowing his reactions and responses slightly, he understood what was being said to him and had no difficulty in recalling and describing recent events. But in that confession he denied he had searched the house, even though police found seat cushions from the settee and armchairs in the living-room pulled off. He did not mention beating Mr Murray with a piece of wood, which had been found heavily bloodstained and which may have caused the marks on the dead man's forehead and chest. He did not mention pressing that piece of wood, or something similar, on to the man's throat. He insisted that the man was 'already cut'. He did not mention squeezing the man's scrotum with his hand (transfer bloodstains had been found suggesting this). He said he had not seen the knife mentioned by the night-watchman.

As a confession it hardly seems exhaustive. In fact, there does not seem to be enough in it to display any special knowledge of the crime. He hit Mr Murray with the 'brick', he said, and the man hit the toilet and fell. He did not say where he got the 'brick', which was not really a brick at all but a piece of building-block. Johnstone could have seen this piece of concrete in the toilet bowl and noticed that the bowl was smashed and perhaps assumed the rest. But there is some doubt as to whether Mr Murray would have hit his head on the way down.

Flecks of blood were found on Johnstone's clothing and more on his shoes, but these could have been picked up while he was trying to apply first-aid. At any rate, had he committed those grotesque acts on Mr Murray's body, we might have expected there to be considerably more. Bloody fingerprints and a handprint found in the house were not matched with his prints. Similarly, bloody fingerprints found on the piece of wood, the carpet knife – which turned out to be yellow and not blue as the night-watchman had first stated – and a bottle of rum discovered in the garden were not matched.

And finally, apart from the allegation of a fight with 'a Paki', which could not be substantiated, there was no reason given by the prosecution as to how he received a three-inch cut on his left thigh. He did not say Mr Murray fought back. And the doctor who examined him said the injury was consistent with 'climbing over a wall or window where there was a sharp projection'. So where did he get it? We'll come to that later.

But if his confession was false, why did he give it? As Dr Gisli H. Gudjonsson, senior lecturer in clinical psychology at London's Institute of Psychiatry points out in his paper, 'The Psychology of False Confessions', people confess to crimes for all manner of reasons, most obviously because they are actually guilty. However, a false confession can be made because the interviewee thinks it is what the police want to hear. Sometimes they do it because they want to get some peace from the constant questioning, a way of avoiding the stress inherent in a police interview. They do not realise the trouble they are getting themselves into and, some-times, retracting the confession later is not enough to get them out of that trouble. Sometimes they do it because, for a variety of reasons, the person is easily suggestible and during questioning they come to believe – or are led to believe – that their recollection of events is wrong and they did, in fact, commit the crime.

If he did not actually murder Mr Murray, who can say why Derek Johnstone confessed early that morning. Perhaps in his drink-and-drug-fogged, sleep-starved brain he felt he really did commit murder. But afterwards he denied it. He said he could not remember even being in the police station, let alone being questioned on tape. He could not remember giving blood, hair and urine samples (although the officer recording these samples failed to note the latter).

And he gave his (new) solicitor, John Carroll, a fresh version of events that night, explaining how he received that wound on his leg. He said that in the early hours of the morning he had planned to break into the town's chemist shop in a bid to obtain more drugs. But when he got there he saw police officers hanging around so he decided against it. Instead, he smashed the window of a newsagent's and climbed inside, slicing his leg open on a shard of glass. He managed to grab some plastic toys from the store before he heard the officers approaching and he squeezed out again, running down the road and hiding in a white Yugo car until they went by. He took a sock off and wrapped it round his leg to staunch the blood.

For this to be true, it would have had to have happened between his leaving his friend's house at 2.30 a.m. and knocking on the elderly lady's door at 2.45 a.m. and asking for a plaster. The following morning, she found the sock on her doorstep, although she was adamant that what she found was a balaclava. The prosecution suggested that had she let Johnstone in, then she might have been murdered instead of Mr Murray.

Police confirmed that there had been a break-in at the shop in question, but they timed the report at between 4.45 a.m. and 5.00 a.m. and said the hole in the glass was not wide enough for anyone to squeeze into. However, a civilian who was passing by the shop at between 1.30 a.m. and 2.00 a.m. said he heard the alarm ringing then, while the glazier who repaired the glass said the hole was three foot by two foot wide, certainly large enough for someone to crawl through. And the owner of the white Yugo confirmed that his car was broken into that night. Nothing was taken but he had found two or three plastic toys in the back which had not been there before. He threw them away. A neighbour said she thought she had heard a bang at about one in the morning. The car break-in was never reported to the police.

Johnstone had known about the newsagent break-in shortly after his arrest. He asked a uniformed officer if he would be set free if he told them about another crime, finally saying that two other boys had committed the crime. Both these boys denied any involvement. So how did Johnstone know about the smashed window and the white Yugo if he had not been there? And by 4.50 a.m., when police say they received the report of the break-in, he was already being questioned about the murder.

170

So, assuming Johnstone was now finally telling the truth, what happened after he left the old lady's house at around 3.00 a.m.? From there on he reverted – to an extent – to the first statement he made to police. He said he made his way to Blackmuir Place, where he heard a noise coming from Samuel Murray's house. But then came an important change to the tale. Originally he said he saw two men running away through the gardens, supplying a fairly detailed description. But now he said the two men left Mr Murray's house and came down the path towards him – and this time he named them. He said they were covered in blood and one of them warned him that if he told anyone he had seen them there, he was a dead man. They then climbed into a car waiting at the kerb and drove off. Then Johnstone went into the house and was subsequently discovered by the night-watchman as he tried to help the old man.

After receiving notification from John Carroll, the police interviewed the two named persons. They spoke to them for about ten minutes each, basically asking them why Derek Johnstone would incriminate them. The men said they were nowhere near the house that night. The police say their fingerprints were checked against those found in the house but, again, no match was made.

What seems to be certain is that Johnstone spoke to the elderly widow at just after 2.45 a.m., stayed approximately a quarter of an hour, and was then found at just after 3.00 a.m. by the night-watchman. That would have given him only a matter of minutes to walk to Blackmuir Place – drunk, drugged and with an injured leg – get into the house and then carry out the horrors against Mr Murray. Given the range of injuries, it remains to be seen if it was possible to inflict them in that time scale. But there is even a problem with the exact time when the call was received from the night-watchman. The civilian operator at Stirling headquarters has said the call was received at 2.45 a.m., the timing taken manually from a 24-hour digital clock display in front of him. But the operator at Alloa police said the call was not received by them until 3.15 a.m., while the first officers on the scene received the message at 3.10 a.m., arriving at 3.20 a.m.! Clearly somebody has their timing wrong. Meantime, a civilian had phoned police at 3.15 a.m. complaining of someone banging at her door. This would have been Johnstone, trying to get help.

But the prosecution was adamant. Johnstone had killed Mr Murray with the intention of robbing him (the bottle of rum was mentioned while a pack of cigarettes allegedly belonging to the old man was found on the boy), but once he had started to attack him he was 'compelled to continue, apparently in order to fulfil incomprehensible urges'. He was found beside the body, the pattern on the sole of his boots apparently matched the bruising pattern on the deceased's chest and he had confessed.

The defence was equally as adamant. He could not have committed such terrible acts in the time available, the bruising pattern on the chest was not necessarily that of his boots but could be the marks left by the edge of the piece of wood and he retracted his confession, which was made while he was under the influence. He did not even recall making it.

In the end, the jury believed the prosecution case and Johnstone was sentenced to life. The main problems facing his defence were his constantly changing stories and his confession.

So, either Johnstone did it and we can all sleep safely in our beds knowing that a monster is safely behind bars, or he did not and he is doing time for a crime committed by someone else. Or, just as disturbingly, maybe he was there, but the assault was committed by others – and those others are still walking around free.

Johnstone is now serving out his time in Dumfries Prison. He continues to maintain his innocence. Attempts to trace witnesses who apparently saw him talking to two men outside the house have so far proved unsuccessful.

And the questions remain unanswered.

SHADOWS AND DOUBTS

For years the Scottish authorities sat smugly in their leather-bound chairs in the darkest recesses of Edinburgh offices, congratulating themselves that their legal system had been free from the ravages inflicted on its English counterpart by a spate of well-publicised miscarriages of justice – a number of cases with handy, headline-friendly names that read like the football pools – Guildford Four, Birmingham Seven, Cardiff Three, Tottenham Two.

But in Scotland these things could not happen, they reassured the public. Our system differs from the English one. We have the corroboration rule, for one thing, which means that people cannot be convicted on a confession alone. But what they forgot to tell that public was that, at least as far as many members of the legal profession is concerned, the corroboration rule has been so eroded over the past 25 years that it has become something of a joke. As one senior police officer from an English force stated to the Royal Commission examining potential changes to the English legal system, corroboration in Scotland can simply be a dog sniffing in the right direction.

Juries, of course, are deemed to be masters of the facts. These 15 citizens, chosen at random, try the accused and find him or her guilty or otherwise – not the police, the prosecution or the judiciary. But, as we have seen in some of the cases detailed in this book, that jury, as a whole, might not be completely certain of guilt. In Scotland, guilt can be determined by a simple majority. That means if eight out of the 15 vote for guilty, then the accused can go to prison for life. But that leaves seven jurors who were, perhaps, not convinced. To some, this calls into question that guilt has been decided beyond a reasonable doubt. Others say that each juror who votes guilty has had to be satisfied beyond a reasonable doubt. The majority rule applies to the weight of the entire jury, therefore if eight of them are satisfied as to guilt then the majority is satisfied beyond that reasonable doubt. But a majority of one still seems pretty slim, even if it is democracy in action. (In England, a majority is ten to two.)

However, the Scottish establishment still insisted that there had been no major miscarriages in Scotland. There was the Oscar Slater case, of course, which proved the need for a Court of Appeal, but that was so long ago. And the papers which proved just how far that particular conspiracy went were not made public until 1994. The Paddy Meehan case was the next big case, but Meehan was pardoned – basically saying we know you did it but we forgive you – and the subsequent inquiry failed to fully clear his name. But Meehan did not murder Mrs Ross, we know that even if, at the time, the courts did not. There were other, smaller, cases, but nobody's perfect. The integrity of the system remained intact.

And it still does, despite a number of other suspect cases which have managed to grab headlines. Thomas Campbell and

Joseph Steele, convicted of murdering six members of one family during the so-called Glasgow Ice-Cream Wars of 1984; Raymond Gilmour, found guilty in 1982 of raping and murdering schoolgirl Pamela Hastie; George Beattie, sentenced to life for the killing of Margaret McLaughlin in Carluke in 1972; Alexander Hall, the brother of murdered George Hall, convicted of cutting the throat of Lorna Porter in Bellshill in 1984; Craig McKenzie, found guilty of helping in the murder of a friend in 1993; William Gray, convicted with James O'Rourke, of murdering Neil Cairney in Airdrie in 1992; John McClay, who was sentenced to life for the stabbing of taxi-driver Stephen McDermott in Glasgow in 1992. There are others, perhaps too many for comfort. All of them have what appear to be valid grounds for questioning their convictions.

Perhaps not all of these men are innocent. But perhaps they are. However, at the time of writing, none of them can have their cases referred back to the Scottish courts, although attempts are being made by family, friends and lawyers. To have them referred back, they are told, there must be additional evidence which was not available at the time of the original trial – and the definition of what constitutes additional evidence in Scotland is tighter than a hangman's noose. We do not have the luxury of the English unsafe and unsatisfactory verdict, which means that the verdict based on the evidence in the case, with the benefit in hindsight, was somehow found wanting. In Scotland – which was once described by a German law student as a first world country with a third world legal system – the only hope for men who have already run the gauntlet of investigation, trial and appeal is for their lawyers or supporters to uncover something that was not known, *or could not have been known*, at the time of the trial. Admissions of perjury by Crown witnesses are not enough. Detailed destruction of the investigation methods is not enough. A confession by another is not enough. For the courts to hear the case again, the evidence must be new. And that is not just difficult, it is nigh on impossible.

(In February 1995, a decision of the Appeal Court chaired by Lord Justice General Lord Hope, Scotland's most senior judge, seemed to open the door to a relaxation of this view, when he allowed certain evidence which was technically available at the time of the original trial. But within a week, other judges appeared to be questioning the ruling, saying that the entire matter would need to be re-examined, and the matter considered by a bench of five judges, before any general loosening of the regulations were carried out. They then refused an appeal in another case lodged on the same basis as the first case, effectively closing the door which Lord Hope had opened.)

As one well-known Glasgow solicitor has said, our law, as interpreted by our judges, relieves them of the obligation of recognising miscarriages of justice even when staring them in the face. Supporters of some of the cases mentioned above – and others – have now banded together to form an umbrella group to campaign en masse.

As these words are being written, the Sutherland Committee is looking at the Scottish system to determine whether a body is needed to investigate alleged miscarriages of justice and to decide whether decisions for new appeals should be taken out of the hands of the politicians – and even the Appeal Court itself. Such a body, albeit not perfect, has already been announced for England and Wales. The Scottish committee's findings are not due to be made public until well into 1996. The umbrella group campaigning for justice for their men can save them a lot of time and public money. They can tell them that we do need an independent body not only to investigate but also to consider these cases.

And we need it now.

Bibliography

Dowdall, Laurence, and Marshall, Alasdair, *Get Me Dowdall* (Paul Harris Publishing), 1979

Fido, Martin, *Murder Guide to London* (Weidenfeld and Nicolson), 1986

Gaute, J.H.H. and Odell, Robin, *Murderer's Who's Who* (Pan), 1980

Gaute, J.H.H. and Odell, Robin, *Murder Whatdunnit* (Pan), 1982

Glaister, John, *Final Diagnosis* (Hutchinson and Co), 1964

Grant, Douglas, *The Thin Blue Line* (John Long), 1973

Knox, Bill, *Court of Murder* (John Long), 1968

Lane, Brian, *The Encyclopaedia of Forensic Science* (Headline), 1992